SANATAN DHARMA
THE LAW OF ETERNITY

BY SADGURU SRI SRI ARJUN

ENGLISH VERSION BY
RABINDRANATH MOHANTY

INDIA · SINGAPORE · MALAYSIA

ISBN
Paperback 979-8-89519-823-0
Hardcase 979-8-89544-879-3

SADGURU SRI SRI ARJUN (1933-1989)

This work is dedicated to Sadguru Sri Sri Arjun

"If you want to be free from sins, change your mind. Because when the mind changes everything else changes. It is ignorance that breeds sins. Sins breed sufferings. Therefore acquire the light of knowledge to dispel the darkness of ignorance. If you want to live, be dutiful; if you want peace and happiness, possess divine qualities; if you want liberation, acquire self-knowledge. Without self-knowledge, liberation is impossible. You have forgotten your Self which means you have lost your Self. Regain your lost paradise. You are forever immortal and free."

Prayer

Oh lord!

Oh indweller of our hearts!

Oh knower of our inner feelings!

You move along,

Wherever our sights tend towards,

Also beyond and still beyond…

You are the lord of life.

You have created this universe.

The ignorant man comprehends nothing.

Being caught up in the snares of ignorance,

He suffers and wails throughout his life.

Oh ruler of our hearts!

In this divine creation,

Your consciousness alone shines out,

But man fails to figure out.

Give us divine knowledge,

Give us knowledge on devotion,

Let the mind and vital energy be fixed on you.

Let this be our prayer always.

Oh lord! The ruler of our hearts!

Original in Oriya- By Sadguru Sri Sri Arjun

Contents

Foreword

It is the changeless and timeless Law that is ever functional regulating the process of generation, operation and dissolution of the universe. When there was no creation, there was only Brahman, who being the supra- causal entity manifests as the creation from subtle to gross by His greatness in a systematic and perfectly synchronized manner taking care of our all-time needs.

The Law of Eternity cannot be comprehended by the people with limited spiritual knowledge. It is beyond human manoeuvres or intellectual interpretations. The Law of Eternity is beginningless and endless too. This is why it is appropriately termed as eternal, as eternal as Brahman. Whatever we come across in this universe are all well planned and well-integrated to ensure a happy and harmonious living and purposeful advancement towards self-realization. Everything has emanated from Brahman. In other words, everything is a manifested form of Brahman. Through an incessant process of transformations, everything shall be merged with Brahman, the unitary, infinite and eternal Existence. Brahman being all-pervasive, all beings are held together and hence all beings are inter-connected. In other words, there is a homogeneous Reality ever-present in all apparent heterogeneities. The divine principles by which Brahman manifests as one and all is known as The Law of Eternity or the Sanatan Dharma which is involved in everything starting from the subtle to the gross, from the insentient to the sentient, from the plants to the planets, from matters to the humans and from the tiny creature to the mighty creation visible and invisible. Sanatan Dharma covers all thoughts, names and forms, intelligence, mind and senses. In other words, it pervades both inner nature and outer nature. Sanatan Dharma can't be comprehended by intellectual exercise for it is beyond the senses, mind and intellect.

Sadguru Sri Sri Arjun says, "Knowing the Law of Eternity is knowledge and observing the same is Dharma. Dharma comes from knowledge and liberation from Dharma."

Sanatan Dharma is a much discussed but most misunderstood term now-a-days. With the passage of time, spiritual knowledge has almost lost its priority in the present society. The prevailing practices on the pretext of religiosity have not been able to offer solace to the suffering people. Rather opposite things are on the rise. We have hardly any time to sit and ponder over wherefrom we came and where shall we go. Hardly there is any time to think about who made the creation in such a well-organized manner making all provisions including space, air, fire, water and earth for all of us. Who created space studded with uncountable twinkling stars and planets, luxuriant plants laden with colourful flowers and fruits enriched with all vitamins and minerals? Who infused consciousness and energy into us and provided oxygen for our breathing? Who designed different bodies with all appropriate accessories for our survival? Who created the tiniest god particles and the colossal black holes, the nuclei and the nebulae? Definitely there is an all-pervasive, ever-operative and uniformly effective divine Law behind all such happenings including all thoughts and all gross and subtle manifestations. That is the divine Sanatan Dharma otherwise termed as the Law of Eternity. By this Law, the root moves deeper into the soil to suck the essential ingredients, the seed germinates and grows to a full-fledged tree, the water turns into vapour and forms the cloud which again comes back to us as rain. Following this Law the Sun and the Earth are constantly engaged in their respective tasks. Following this Law, different organs of our bodies truthfully operate. These are mere hints but the list is endless indeed.

All scriptures have repetitively harped on this theme of Advait which means non-dualism. Sadguru Sri Sri Arjun (1933-1989), preached his philosophy titled Divya Darshan {The Philosophy Divine) and lucidly explained Sanatan Dharma that regulates the great cycle from creation to dissolution embracing in its fold one and all without exception.

We place on record our profuse appreciation of this compilation by Sri Rabindranath Mohanty, the President of Divya Darshan Sangha who has come forward to spread Sadguru's teachings on Sanatan Dharma in a very concise and comprehensive manner so as to reach the humanity irrespective of caste, creed and religiosities. We trust, this handy book shall be well- received by our readers.

Central Committee

Divya Darshan Sangha

Co-operative Colony

Rayagada – 765001

18th July 2024 (Guru Jayanti)

Sadguru Sri Sri Arjun (1933-1989)

His Holiness Sadguru Sri Sri Arjun (1933-1989), was born on 18.07.1933 at Gudiabandh (a village near Gunupur of Rayagada District in Odisha) to Sri Odiya Gomango and Srimati Chandrama Devi. His original name was Arjun Gomango.

He had studied up to class VIII in Gunupur High school of Koraput Dist (Odisha). He was very intelligent with an analytical mind and inquisitiveness with excellent grasping capacity. He had a strong inclination towards science and technical studies. But he was not interested in the routine syllabus-bound school education. He was good in carpentry, drawing, dance, music, painting, sculpting, drama, astrology, palmistry, Ayurveda and magic etc.

After his school education, he underwent training on Turner trade at ITI, Cuttack, but could not complete the course. He worked as carpentry teacher at different schools of Koraput district for about 7 years. Then he set up a furniture shop and electric appliance repair shop. From 1967, he worked at HAL Sunabeda till his demise in 1989.

Once while reading a science book, he came across a topic on X-ray. A scientist had written, "On passing electricity through a vacuumed tube, he had observed a feeble ray inside the tube. He could not cognize it fully. But he had a conviction that there was a fourth state of matter." This term, "fourth state of matter" made Him inquisitive. There are normally three states of matter, i.e. solid, liquid and gaseous. The fourth state, if any, is not discussed or clearly comprehended. He started inquiring into the fourth state of matter. He had tremendous respect for knowledge. Once his mind was inclined towards fourth state of matter, he got inclined towards the subtlest subject of spirituality. He reasoned that, behind the changeable Creation, there is some unchangeable and independent power. This thought haunted him again and again. All his previously nurtured obsessions slowly vanished. He became keen to know about the Eternal Truth.

In the year 1948, when he was 15 year old, he came across **Socrates**' words; "Ignorance is a great sin." At that time he was a student of class VIII. This statement spontaneously triggered an awakening in him. He accepted Socrates as his spiritual master (Guru). He heartily concurred with this statement of Socrates and repeated the same several times as if it was a great *mantra* for him. He was convinced that by acquiring knowledge only, ignorance could be dispelled. That means, not acquiring knowledge is a sin. Sins are committed due to ignorance. By welcoming divinity, man can get rid of all sins and attain divinity. By knowledge only man can raise himself to a greater height, i.e. to the stage of Supreme. The divine knowledge is therefore essential.

In 1963, while going through the Bible, he was greatly impressed with the teachings of **Jesus Christ** and accepted him as his Guru. "Ask, you will get; Seek, it will be revealed; Knock, the door shall be opened." These sermons of Jesus inspired him to ask, seek and knock which were essential for any seeker of knowledge to go further and further.

In 1965, he happened to come across **Buddha's** teachings. Buddha had envisioned sorrows and sufferings everywhere. Sorrow is entangled with birth and death. Sorrow is there with decay or disease. Sorrows according to him follow everyone just as the wheels of the bullock cart follow the hooves of the bullocks. According to Buddha there are four noble truths. First, there is suffering. Second, there is a cause behind the origin of suffering. Third, suffering which has come shall also go. Fourth, as there is a cause for the suffering, there is also a cause for its cessation. Once the cause is known the sufferings shall vanish. He stated that, "Craving is the cause of sufferings." Annihilation of cravings will lead to cessation of sufferings. Annihilating cravings means extinguishing the fire of desires. That is the state of *Nirvana*. Hence Buddha's first discourse at Sarnath is known as the Fire Discourse. Arjun accepted Lord Buddha as his Guru.

In a nutshell, Socrates represented knowledge and truth; Jesus represented Love and Forgiveness; Buddha represented Truth and non-injury (love). Arjun appreciated and realised the essence of these teachings. He accepted the three masters as his Guru and drew inspiration from their words.

He had also accepted various sages, Vedas and Vedantas, Prakriti and Param Brahman as his Guru. By seeing, hearing and deeply meditating, he could go deep into any subject. Thus out of his seven Gurus, the last Guru is God. God being Omnipresent, Omniscient and Omnipotent, makes everything possible.

He got the insight that the universe is full of energy; knowledge is energy and by knowledge-power all other powers are understood, appreciated and acquired. Whether it is energy or matter, the fourth state of matter must be identical and homogeneous. He developed a conviction that the higher state of consciousness starts from this stage. Why it happens? How it happens? Who is the cause behind all these happenings? All these questions repeatedly haunted him and he started inquiring into these questions.

Normally the scientists who deal with physical science do not believe in God. According to them, the matter is converted to energy and vice versa. This is the natural law which is final, they believe. According to them there is no need to believe in another power called God. There is no such existence as God.

But Sadguru Sri Sri Arjun's thinking was different. He did not want to put a stop to further enquiry. He wanted to unfold things more and more. According to him, it is true that matter is converted to energy and vice versa. But how does this conversion take place? For this process of transformation, there has to be some independent principle, law or some power that is at work. That principle, remaining independent of matter and energy but residing in the matter and energy, must be governing the process of transformation. In other words, there is some external impressed force that remains internally but independently to trigger the process of change from matter to energy and vice-versa. The spiritualists call it God, Brahman, Atman or Self. The energy that is talked about in the domain of physical science is termed by spiritualists as *apara shakti* (lower power). There is still a higher power called *para shakti* which causes and controls *apara shakti*. With such inquisitive mind, he continued with his spiritual pursuits, till he realised the Truth.

He was a house-holder and yet by his persistence inquisitiveness and continuous spiritual practice, attained enlightenment in the year 1967. Post realisation, He propounded his unique philosophy, namely, **Divya Darshan** which focuses on consciousness, knowledge, Truth, love and bliss, other concepts like Theory of Change, Theory of Colours, Theory of Rebirth etc. He established Divya Darshan Sangh and started accepting disciples from 1976. He toured extensively in the interior districts of Odisha to spread the knowledge of Oneness. Divya Darshan stands on three pillars. First, one should do his duties diligently to the best of one's abilities; Second, one should practice divine qualities like *(Thyaga, Sanyama, Sadhana, Seva, Satya, Prema and khyama)* to live harmoniously in society; Third, one must develop an intense longing for self-knowledge which alone will lead to self-realisation. He has shown the path to be a good house-holder; to live in society and at the same time realise ones' Self.

Sadguru Sri Sri Arjun says, "Oh, mankind!

Forgetting your True Self and mistaking this stage for your abode and unreal role for your Self, how long will you continue to be tortured in the frying cauldrons of lust and greed, pride and prejudice?

Arise! Enkindle the flame of awareness within.

Get ready to return to your peaceful, immortal and heavenly abode and get back your eternal, true and pure Self. Then only you will free yourself from all miseries and fears.

Remember! You are immortal and free."

Introduction

Most of us are not aware that we are all governed by a Law called the Law of Eternity. All changes, internal and external are caused and conditioned by this Law. We are also unaware of the Omnipotent Creator who is the maker of this Law. This Law is intended for progress and wellbeing, peace, happiness and bliss of all beings in this Creation. It is everybody's duty to observe this Law to further the Creator's cause. No one is expected to break the Law. The offenders are punished at the appropriate time. There is Law of Karma which comes under the overall purview of the Law of Eternity. Ignorance of this Law and consequent sins bring us sufferings.

The Law of Eternity manifests itself as various lower truths in the physical world cognizance of which comes under the ambit of physical science or scientific truths. Whether it is the law of gravitation, or properties of space, air, fire, water and minerals or the living beings in whom the digestive system, respiratory system, blood circulation system etc. are embedded, all are manifestations of the Law of Eternity. That means those are not man-made. Man must try to comprehend that behind the lower truths operative in the physical planes, there are higher truths, which govern the lower truths. Those higher truths are the prerogatives of the Almighty. In other words, those are God's Will or the manifestations of the Absolute Consciousness. The Absolute Truth manifests as the relative truths in the subtle and gross Creation. God alone is the only Reality.

Every particle in this universe is designed and engaged to serve some purpose or other. While it itself evolves, it also contributes to the process of evolution of the entire Creation in a natural way for an unknown goal. Matter is transformed into energy. Energy is transformed into matter. This process goes on perennially to project a renewed Creation every moment. In other words, everybody consciously or unconsciously undertakes some efforts and everybody is inextricably linked to some pre-set goal.

There is some law governing birth. There is some law governing death. These laws prevail everywhere at all times irrespective of caste creed and culture, irrespective of whether it is South Pole or North Pole. There is a law behind sufferings. There is a law behind happiness. There is a law behind bondage and there is a law behind liberation. This law is timeless and is of universal application. This law is the truth. Knowing this truth is knowledge. Not knowing this truth is ignorance. Ignorance creates illusory effects i.e. *Maya*. It veils the truth and projects it in different ways. The perceivers, because of gradations of knowledge understand things in different ways.

Man is the most developed living being of this Creation. He is endowed with a higher intellect. He understands the underlying essence of everything although he is also steeped in ignorance. He has therefore to acquire the light of knowledge as a result of which the darkness of ignorance can be dispelled. He has to necessarily nurture the divine virtues in him, which will help him realise his goal. The goal is to return to where he has come from. He is on an unknown journey but he is waylaid. The lighthouse of knowledge can show him the right direction to reach his heavenly abode where eternal peace and bliss reign. Hence Divya Darshan says, "To know the Law of Eternity is knowledge and to observe the same is Dharma. Dharma culminates in liberation or total freedom."

Queer ideas about Dharma

Some people say, "I am doing my duty; that is enough. That is Dharma." Some others say, "I am living in a righteous manner. That is Dharma." Whether righteous living can be called as Dharma; whether doing one's duty is Dharma; whether we know what is our duty? Divya Darshan says, righteous living and doing one's duty is not same as Dharma. But they help one move on the path of Dharma.

How to observe Dharma? To understand Dharma one has to acquire Knowledge and practise Divine qualities. One has to acquire knowledge to understand and realise the Truth. After knowing it, one has to observe the Truth in day to day life. When one practises divine qualities like Renunciation, Restraint, Spiritual Practice, Service, Truth, Love and Forgiveness, he gradually gets purified. And in the process he acquires knowledge and realises the various truths governing this Creation and Self. Once he knows about the mechanism of Creation, he starts believing in the omnipotent Existence and accelerates his journey on the path of Dharma.

Swadharma

Many people believe that *swadharma* is the duty bestowed upon a man according to his birth, caste or ancestral practices. *Swadharma* was understood and interpreted correctly in the earlier days but slowly it got enveloped by ignorance. In course of time the correct meaning was distorted. Different persons have interpreted *swadharma* differently. This has led to confusion about the true meaning of *swadharma*. People consider something to be their *Dharma* even though they are indulging in *adharma* while performing their occupational practices. More often than not, people mechanically confine themselves to their *Karma* without knowing the intricacy of Karma but claim to be performing their *swadharma*. Of course some *karma* has to be performed keeping in view the environmental and circumstantial factors but that cannot be claimed as *swadharma*. For example, a butcher may claim that he is performing his *swadharma* while butchering the animals. Scriptures exhort, "Killing animals is a sin". A thief has accepted theft as his occupational pursuit and treats the same as his *swadharma*. In other words, *swadharma* is misused and misunderstood to such an extent that even theft is also talked of as *swadharma* on the lame excuse of maintenance of family. Similarly, mass killing or terrorism is also mistaken as patriotism.

Dharma is generally viewed from two angles. First is behavioural aspect; second is spiritual aspect. *Dharma* in its social, individual or general aspect can be clubbed under behavioural aspect. It also covers moral aspects, mannerisms, and courtesy etc. By practising the above, man generally achieves physical and mental purity and also his devotional inclinations. The divine qualities slowly develop. Right from birth till the stage of sustenance of the body, this behavioural *Dharma* plays its role. That means this behavioural *Dharma* helps one to grow up in a society with harmony and happiness. This leads to spiritual knowledge. Without spiritual knowledge and experience, man cannot realise God's existence and reach the ultimate goal. Therefore, whatever is done for realisation of True Self is *swadharma*. Observance of *swadharma* is the only means of getting God's grace.

Man suffers due to want of knowledge. In other words, without knowing where and what to be done, why to be done, he whimsically imagines a particular event or situation in his own way. More often than not, he is unable to identify the lapses in his karma. This lack of knowledge brings him misery. In order to help mankind dispel ignorance and tide over sufferings, the sages of yesteryears have handed down to us the Vedas, the Upanishads and various other scriptures. Still some superstitions have crept into the behavioural *Dharma*. Due to inadequate knowledge, we are not able to know our own deficiencies. To attain spiritual knowledge, behavioural *Dharma* is necessarily to be observed. This aspect also remains diluted. Due to this, there are hindrances on our ways and we are not able to move faster towards our goal.

It is to be remembered that the word *swadharma* is used to signify all those duties, which are necessary to be performed for realisation of true self. But people do not understand the true meaning of this term as a result of which they resort to wrong practices and consequently suffer. If duty is performed keeping in view the realisation of true self, then *Sanatan Dharma*, is followed in true spirit.

Sanatan Dharma

Sanatan means Eternal. *Dharma* is the universal principle of law, order and truth. It is the regulatory principle of the universe. The sages were aware of the greatness of *Sanatan Dharma* and carefully and consciously named it as such. It means Law of Eternity. That cosmic Law, which is ever-operative, was first realised by the sages and thereafter they called the same as *Sanatan.* The term *Sanatan* is meaningful indeed. *Sanatan Dharma* is ever present and God-made. It is beginningless and endless too. It is not the brainchild of any human being. It is eternal and therefore unamendable.

Dharma is not same as Religion. Religion is not an appropriate substitute for *Dharma,* which has a definite connotation in Sanskrit or other Indian languages whereas the word, 'religion', has its limitations. Many people understand that observance of *Dharma* is nothing but following certain rituals prevalent in the society. Some others feel that *Dharma* is nothing but praying or worshipping God in some particular way. Some consider that *Dharma* lies in doing charity, chanting God's name and undergoing fasting for receiving divine grace.

Many people think that telling truth is *Dharma,* offering sacrifices is *Dharma,* building temples, churches or mosques is *Dharma. Dharma* has been more misunderstood than understood as a result of which many actively indulge in mischiefs in the name of *Dharma,* only for the fulfilment of their selfish desires. It is tragic that *Dharma* has not been understood properly by many. Every one boasts of one's own religion and denounces the other religion. Throughout the world, this feeling of upholding one's own faith and denouncing others' is seen quite often.

It has to be remembered that whatever knowledge the sages have imparted, is nothing but the essence of *Sanatan Dharma*. At different times, those teachings slowly faded into oblivion and therefore partial observance of *Dharma* is seen in some cases. Since we do not have the precise knowledge about *Dharma*, we try to explain *Dharma* by stating that praying God is *Dharma*, Non-violence is *Dharma*, Speaking truth is *Dharma*, Doing one's duty is *Dharma*; Performing some rituals is *Dharma*. But deeper insight into the subject will reveal that these are only means to *Dharma* and not really *Dharma*. Real *Dharma* is something else, far above all these.

Scriptures prescribe that sufferings shall vanish by observing *Dharma*. But the chain of sufferings, indicates that we do not really practise *Dharma* rather we practise *adharma* (opposite to *Dharma*) mistaking the same for *Dharma*.

Whatever is seen in the realm of nature, whatever changes are perceived in nature by way of creation, preservation and destruction and whatever we come across like Sun, Moon, and Planets. Stars, animals, plants etc. in the process of change are definitely caused and conditioned by someone. In other words, there is definitely some causal factor behind all these. There are laws to accomplish the process. The Law governs all changes, the effect of which we see as the gross objects or the visible world.

To be clear, there are some laws for the creation; there are some laws for preservation and also there are some laws for destruction. Nothing is possible without these Laws. For example, a plant to survive, to bear flowers and fruits, to develop seeds and again for seeds to grow into plants, some pre-existing laws are at work. Similarly the roots of the tree go deep and suck food from the soil for sustenance. In the animal kingdom also, certain laws or principles govern birth, growth, procreation, decay and death. These aspects are called as properties or *Dharma*. The properties are embedded in all matters. That is expressed as *Dharma* of a particular matter. The properties of water are different from those of fire. Since the properties are different in different matters, they are identified as such. Every birth presupposes some definite purpose.

Eternally governed by this Law of Eternity, everything, maintaining its relative identity for some period, changing its relative identity in course of time and depending upon its latent qualities, also undergo changes in course of time, evolves and advances towards a common goal, which is beyond all relativities and hence absolute and real. The so-called imperfections we come across all around are but passing phases in a grand process that ends up as a perfect, indivisible and homogeneous unity. We are unable to cognize the great Law involved in this consciously energized evolutionary process.

What is *Dharma* and what is the purpose behind *Dharma*? Unless we know what Dharma is, we may not be in a position to observe *Dharma* in a flawless manner. In this phenomenal world, we find that everything has a beginning as well as end. Everybody passes through various stages between its beginning and end so as to reach his ultimate goal. Everybody is to reach there where they had come from.

Water becomes vapour and again drops down as rain and mingles in the ocean. Seed becomes a tree, bears fruits and flowers and again becomes seed. This type of cycle is undergone by everyone. While these are all individual cycles, there is another grand cycle at work encompassing all individual cycles. This grand cycle is nothing but creation from Brahman and immergence in Brahman. Whatever manifests from Brahman will be merged with Brahman. The Law that governs the grand cycle is the Law of Eternity.

Sanatan Dharma means the basic principles involved in the manifestation and play of Brahman. Brahman is without any beginning and without any end. Everything is created from Him and merges with Him. This process continues eternally. Hence, where is the beginning, or where is the end? That is why this Law is *Sanatan,* meaning eternal. This Law has created everything. This Law regulates everything. From creation to the ultimate end i.e. immergence with Brahman, everything i.e. form, quality, jiva, plants and matter etc. comes under *Sanatan Dharma.*

The observance of *Dharma* gives rise to peace, happiness and liberation. Impulses acquired in the previous births form the basis of life in the next births. For the preservation and ultimate end of any creation or any form that comes into existence, certain qualities or properties are present in everything. These properties sustain the container, protect and ultimately lead towards its dissolution. This is called *Mukti* or liberation. In other words, to attain Brahman or true self, or to get rid of sufferings is called *Mukti* or liberation. Had this not been there, nothing would have existed. It would not have been possible to experience anything, had there been no process of creation and ultimate journey to Brahman.

The sages had realised the mystery of the creation but the ignorant man is unable to understand the grand purpose behind the creation. Man is not born only to survive, eat and enjoy.

Had it been so, it would have been sufficient to remain as animals without evolving to manhood. There is definitely a specific purpose behind human birth. Man can understand and appreciate things better than animals. What is more, God has endowed man with inquisitiveness. By this inquisitiveness, man would slowly realise everything, get peace and happiness and ultimately realise Brahman. This is evident from the fact that every human being instinctively wants peace, happiness, bliss and freedom. To attain all these He has assumed the human form, which is said to be much sought after by the Devas even. For the sustenance of his body, it is necessary to feed himself. Without food, how can he survive? If he cannot survive, how can he get peace or bliss? He has to survive, get peace and happiness and in the process he will also acquire the knowledge of *Mukti* or knowledge of his True Self.

For that purpose, nature has also made arrangements for his food. Be it the vegetable kingdom or the animal kingdom, all their prerequisites for their existence are provided even before their birth. For that, the five elements such as earth, water, fire, air and ether have been made available. The five elements are designed to contain the required intakes for the vegetable kingdom. Thereafter has evolved the animal kingdom. Thus *Sanatan Dharma* operates in the whole kingdom of nature and fulfils all requirements of each species.

For example, milk creation process starts in the mother's breast after conception but before the birth of the child. This happens so that a baby can live on the mother's milk after its birth. Is it not a wonderful arrangement!

In fact, the body, mind, vital energy, intellect and conscience are very closely interwoven and become functional due to the operation of the Law of eternity. There is no chance of any interruption to this Law of Eternity. This Law regulates the manhood of man, his life, and his vital energy. Man can never isolate himself from this Law. Without this Law, he can never exist. Therefore, it is said, "*Dharma* sustains, protects and ultimately leads one to Liberation". It is sheer ignorance to seek peace, bliss and freedom without observing this Law of eternity. The fact is that happiness, peace, bliss and freedom are embedded in *Sanatan Dharma*.

Scriptures prescribe us the ways of getting peace, bliss and liberation. What is this way? What is Creation and what is its mystery? What is God or Creator? What is freedom or liberation? Who is the jiva? Scriptures teach us about the *Sanatan Dharma*. Veda means knowledge. Whatever the Vedas teach us are the subject matter of *Sanatan Dharma* or the Law of Eternity. Everything in this creation becomes operative by the Law of Eternity. This Law of Eternity is present in everything in this Creation. By this law alone, every movement, every evolution, every development and every accomplishment of life are regulated. To know all these or to know the Law of eternity is true knowledge and observance of the Law of Eternity is true *Dharma*. Without this knowledge life becomes meaningless.

The essence of *Sanatan Dharma* is present more or less in all religions and in all philosophies. In yesteryears, people had sufficient knowledge of *Sanatan Dharma* and they regulated their living accordingly. People were enjoying long life with peace and happiness. They were also preparing themselves for liberation. That supreme knowledge is now confined to books and scriptures without being accessed by common men. Therefore, man suffers. Since we are suffering, it has to be inferred that we are not having the right knowledge or knowledge on *Sanatan Dharma.*

The right knowledge is called knowledge on Brahman, knowledge on Atman, knowledge on Truth, knowledge on True Self, etc. This knowledge is verily divine. He who will acquire this knowledge will become himself divine. He, who will become divine, will definitely attain to divinity, who is Brahman and also his divine True Self.

In this world today, man is beset with fear, miseries and every moment he is seen to be restless and clamouring for peace. From these symptoms, it can be inferred that he is not able to realise the essence of *Sanatan Dharma.* Therefore, instead of developing his divine virtues from within, he has been nurturing the devilish tendencies, which brings sufferings. It is imperative to acquire the divine knowledge pertaining to *Sanatan Dharma.* The present day mankind is awfully lacking in two most important things, namely, divine qualities and divine knowledge.

There is no dearth of temples, mosques and churches. Rather the number is increasing day by day. The number of devotees under various sects and religious faiths is also growing. Simultaneously, the demoniac qualities are also on an increase. Many seem to be getting more and more inclined towards materialism than divine knowledge. The scriptural instructions on divine knowledge are just confined to a few.

Divya Darshan lays utmost emphasis on *Sanatan Dharma,* knowledge and divine qualities, which are essential for attaining peace, bliss and liberation. God expresses Himself as true knowledge and divine qualities. Possessing divine qualities is *Dharma* because only through divine qualities, advancement towards realisation of True Self is possible. In other words, divine qualities are the divine vehicles to divinity, *moksa* or liberation.

Dharma in the Context of Spirituality

[Dharma is one of the most misunderstood words. It is translated as religion in English. Actually religion is not same as Dharma. Further people misunderstand Dharma as a set of rituals or practices. Dharma is also associated with temples, the idols, the priests and the rituals observed. Actually Dharma is not about observing some rituals; it is far beyond that. It is a way of life. Dharma when observed properly leads to self-realisation which is the goal of human life. In fact it is difficult to define Dharma and put a boundary on its meaning and implications. Dharma has been broadly defined as that which always upholds and protects everyone and everything.

We think that doing charity, giving donation, extending social service, to visit temples and worship God, to sing Bhajan, to tell truth, to build schools and hospitals etc. are all Dharma, but these are not Dharma. These are only auxiliary requirements for observance of Dharma. These are all noble deeds one should do but these are not Dharma; these are all means to Dharma. By such acts our antahkaran (internal organs like mind, intellect, chitta and ego) shall get purified.

In the words of Sadguru Sri Sri Arjun, "Where there is Dharma, there is peace and bliss because Dharma protects us, sustains us and liberates us." Sadguru Sri Sri Arjun has explained in simple terms the true meaning of Dharma in the following discourses.]

[1]Man is the best creation of God. Food requirements, fear, sleep, and procreation are the basic nature of all animals. The man also possesses these four characteristics. What is extra in him is his inquisitiveness for knowledge and Dharma. The sages and seers have all along been exhorting mankind to know what Dharma is and how to observe the same. Dharma has been defined as that which always upholds and protects everyone. In some places, the ways to attain Dharma have been prescribed. The sages and seers knew what Dharma is and accordingly they were conducting themselves as a result of which they were getting peace and happiness. But today's man hardly understands the real import of Dharma. Due to ignorance, man is not able to observe Dharma properly. Hence man is getting less peace and more of sufferings. In the name of Dharma, man does perform lots of rituals but still peace remains a far cry. Instances of corrupt practices, falsehood, cheating, brutality and jealousy are on the increase. There are threats of war instead of call for peace. Sadguru Sri Sri Arjun says, "Where there is Dharma, there is peace and bliss because Dharma protects us, sustains us and liberates us."

Sadguru Sri Sri Arjun emphasises on, "Ignorance is the cause of sufferings". Ignorance about Truth and Dharma is the main reason for the disorder and disturbances. Self-realisation is true Dharma.

---

1 Oriya Divya Dhara Vol 1 Page 3

 SANATAN DHARMA

What is Dharma?

It's not easy to speak about Dharma. It is a vast subject dealing with very subtle aspects. Many do not understand what Dharma is. Only sages and seers know the true import of Dharma. Many definitions of Dharma are advanced in the scriptures. Even if volumes of explanations are available in the scriptures, still the people at large fail to understand the true spirit and essence of Dharma due to ignorance and lack of interest.

We talk of Sanatan Dharma. But to whom the word Sanatan is ascribed, we do not know. The wise men interpret that whatever exists always and that which is beginningless and endless, is Sanatan Dharma. The eternal law that governs always is called the Law of Eternity. But the question is what exists always? What is that Law that is always operative? Since we do not know the basis of all these, we are not able to tell correctly about Dharma. We say that we are walking the path of Dharma but we make so many deviations. The truth is- "Wherever there is Dharma, there is peace; wherever there is Dharma, there is bliss; wherever there is Dharma, there is *Mukti* or Freedom."

Now the question is, when we do not get peace, bliss and freedom, then what type of Dharma are we observing? If we are not in peace and bliss, then how shall we get liberation (*Mukti*) or freedom? We must understand that *Mukti* is a state of mind where there is no fear, no suffering, no doubt and no anxiety. Since we are having all of these, it is quite evident that we are not moving towards liberation. Had we really progressed towards liberation, these negative symptoms would have waned away slowly. All these persisting negative symptoms expose not only our ignorance but also non-observance of actual Dharma.

We merely know that charity (to donate some amount or to extend some services), to worship God, to tell truth and to have devotion are all Dharma. But these are not Dharma. These are only auxiliary requirements for observance of Dharma. These are all means to Dharma. To make sacrifices, to dig wells and ponds are noble works which should be undertaken but these are means to Dharma only. Then the question is- what else Dharma is?

Generally, if somebody undertakes some pious works, we call him Dharmic. Even people who undertake different occupations treat their occupations as their Dharma or *karttavya*. In that case what shall we speak of a butcher? Is killing animals his duty or Dharma? Scriptures exhort us to practise non-injury. "Do not steal, do not tell lies, do not grab others' properties, do not think ill of others," thus instruct the scriptures. Hence whatever occupations we undertake may not be on the tracks of Dharma.

Dharma takes us on the path of self-purification or self-development, peace and bliss. Some people consider that their path of Dharma or their religion is the best. But after knowing the real meaning of Dharma, one would not say that any particular religion is superior and the other inferior. Dharma is always Dharma. Dharma is eternal.

We follow different traditions and practices on the pretexts of our religious obligations. But what exactly Dharma is, we do not know. There are some social laws which are followed due to local rules and practices. Our cultural activities, festivities and different types of social traditions are carried out in different manners according to local practices. These cannot be called eternal laws. These are only practices which are subject to change over a period of time. These practices are developed and being followed for a good and harmonious social living, but they are not eternal. Many traditions die down in course of time. The new generation may not have respect towards such age-old practices if those are unscientific, irrational or redundant. Slowly many old traditions fade into oblivion. Those social systems are man-made. When situations, circumstances or social priorities change, they also undergo suitable modifications or at times, conveniently bypassed.

But the Law of Eternity is observed always irrespective of time and place. The Sages of yesteryears knew what Sanatan Dharma or the eternal Dharma is. When we do not know what Sanatan Dharma is, how can we assert that we are observing Dharma?

Had we really known what Dharma is, we would not have suffered. We also do not know how to observe Dharma. The subject matter of Dharma, more often than not, remains confined to spiritual texts. Unless knowledge is acquired, Dharma cannot be understood in totality. In absence of knowledge, we construe the social laws, traditions and different racial or local practices for Dharma. We remain complacent with observing some rituals. There are some ethical practices or prescriptions developed in course of time for bringing discipline in the society. Courtesy, morality, good qualities such as respect, non-stealing and non-injury are considered to be parts of Dharma. These are all required for the well-being of human beings. These qualities create a healthy environment in the society to live in peace and happiness. But these are all auxiliary requirements for the observance of Dharma. We are ignorant about the essence or true nature of Dharma. To tell truth is Sanatan Dharma. To love others is Sanatan Dharma. Lord Jesus said, "Love thy neighbour as thyself." Buddha preached *ahimsa* or non-injury to others.

By violent means this Creation shall be destroyed. By non-violence and love the Creation can flourish. Sense of love is also present everywhere even in lower creatures, insects and plants.

Love is divine. That love appears in different situations differently such as- love between husband and wife, love between father and son, love between mother and child, brother and sister etc. Had there been no love we would have always quarrelled with each other. This Creation would not have been there. Due to love a tigress takes care of her cubs. In case of human beings, after a child takes birth, his mother brings him up by taking lot of care. She educates the child, takes care for his well-being, and always thinks well of him. The animal kingdom would not have existed without love. For the animal kingdom to exist there are some divine qualities such as renunciation, service and love etc. These divine qualities are the divine provisions in the Law of Eternity that takes care of everyone in the Creation. When husband returns from his work place to residence, his wife keeps food ready, for she knows that her husband would come at a specified time. Any deviation from this truth would create disturbance and misunderstanding. Further without a spirit of sacrifice, no one can help another person. The divine qualities are already effective in the kingdom of nature as a result of which we see this orderly Creation. Deviations cause distortions and disturbances. In all sects or religions, importance is attached to the divine qualities. It is said that God becomes happy to see His children helping each other and sacrificing for each other. By divine qualities the Creation gets sweetened by peace, happiness and bliss. These divine qualities are the essential requirement for attaining the goal. In our society due to superstitions, we offer animal sacrifices to propitiate God. But the sages and scriptures had taught non-injury to animals. That means, we are doing *Adharma* in the name of Dharma due to want of proper knowledge about Dharma. By possessing divine qualities man can earn peace and happiness. By divine qualities he can move on the path of self-development and realise his true nature. The opposite qualities of divine qualities are demoniac qualities which impede the progress of man towards self-realisation as a result of which peace and happiness remain far away from him. In the name of Dharma, due to ignorance, we arouse the demoniac qualities in us. We are killing animals like goats, cows, buffaloes etc. Where is Dharma in these types of practices? Are we supposed to eat animals also? Whatever gives us peace and happiness and accelerates our journey towards self-development, and ultimately self-realisation is called Dharma. In other words, virtues lead us to self-development while the sins or vices drag us to sufferings. There is Dharma in virtues, *Adharma* in vices. We are bound to suffer because we are doing *Adharma* under the pretext of Dharma. Suffering is entwined with *Adharma*. Happiness is entwined with virtues. Because people do not know this, they steal on the one hand and donate big amounts to God on the other hand. They feel complacent after donating as they think that they are sacrificing for God.

God will be happy to see our devotion, and not the vulgar display of our wealth and properties. Some people take pride in carrying out different types of worships and getting themselves tortured by not taking any food or water even. To propitiate God there is no need at all to do any such penances. According to Ayurveda, the following four categories of people such as children, patients or weak persons, pregnant women and old persons should not undertake any fasting. But we do fast on different occasions and feel satisfied that we have performed our dharmic duties. This human body is a gift of God. It is our first and foremost duty to take care of the body. Then only we can do all the virtuous deeds. It is further mentioned in the scriptures that those who are healthy, they can fast once in a fortnight or twice in a month. If someone fasts, he should take plenty of water. There are many other injunctions in the scriptures on intake of food. One should not take non-veg food along with milk and ghee. One should not take meat and fish together. Blood will become impure if one takes food in such odd combinations. One should follow all scriptural guidelines which are meant for maintenance of the body. If we omit to take care of this fundamental duty, how shall we get peace and happiness?

The second requirement is that man must live harmoniously in society. There are certain principles to be followed for living in the society with peace and happiness. Those are all our social duties and responsibilities, but we neglect in this area also.

We should always be humble and respectful to others. If we are arrogant there will always be quarrel or heated arguments with others. How can we get peace possessing the qualities of selfishness, arrogance and jealousy etc.? Due to ignorance we suffer. Even due to jealousy, our sufferings get multiplied due to the growing happiness of our neighbours. At times, people go to temples only to pray for the ill of others. By any definition, this cannot be called devotion. Man must try to acquire knowledge and broaden his vision. Man should approach a Sadguru to learn different aspects of life such as duty, righteousness, truth and goal of life. One should at least read some scriptures that the sages have handed down to us. Man seeks peace and happiness.

This would not come from cheating others. There are many virtuous ways to get happiness. We should learn those ways. Why man seeks peace and happiness? What is the purpose of this human birth? What is Dharma? What is the goal of life?

If a man does not know the answers to the above questions, it means, he does not know what Dharma is. Hence there would be lapses in observance of Dharma.

A person should ask himself, "Why is he taking food?" The common reply would be - "To survive."

Why is a man so keen to survive? If we do not know the answer, it is to be understood that we do not know what Dharma is. Dharma includes every dimension of our life. If we are not clear about the fundamental aspects of our lives, this means we do not know what Dharma is; we also do not observe Dharma. We simply follow some rituals or social practices blindly in the name of Dharma.

With such mindset, we are bound to suffer. Dharma only can lead us to peace and happiness. Observance of Dharma will lead to cessation of sins and sufferings. We commit different kinds of lapses in absence of knowledge about Dharma.

There are ways to get peace and happiness. There are also ways to get freedom or liberation.

Dharma explained

- Whatever is done for maintenance of the body is Dharma.

- Whatever is done to live harmoniously in the society with peace and happiness is Dharma.

- Whatever is done to attain self-development and the goal of self-realisation is Dharma.

The law governing the above three points is known as the Law of Eternity. The food is different for different animals. Accordingly, their physical structures and systems are different. Nature has designed them accordingly. All these are governed by the Law of Eternity. The sages have envisioned this Law and exhorted mankind to observe the Law for maintenance of body, for happy and peaceful social living and ultimately for self-realisation. This Law is eternally operative. The same Law was applicable in the past to the animals and to the plant kingdom. Now also the same Law is applicable and in future too the same Law will be applicable. Everything is there in the kingdom of nature. We see the mineral kingdom, plant kingdom and the animal kingdom. This has been possible due to the Law of Eternity. Our existence, peace and happiness and ultimately liberation are all governed by the Law of Eternity. He, who consciously observes this Law, can speed up his journey to bliss and liberation. For that, first we must know what that Law of Eternity is. But due to ignorance, we are not able to know the indispensability of the Law of Eternity and are not keen to observe the same. We know a few things. That is why we are able to survive, maintain our bodies and live in the society with some peace and happiness. But we do not know how to get freedom. Overall, we do not have knowledge of Dharma. Whatever we know is very little and partial. With the scant and scattered knowledge that we have, we are under a wrong notion that we are observing Dharma.

We also do not evince interest to know more about Dharma. Divya Darshan says that if one does not acquire knowledge, one cannot know Dharma. By knowledge only one can distinguish between Dharma and *Adharma*. With the help of knowledge only we come to know what nectar is and what poison is. A small kid may swallow poison without slightest hesitation. He may also put his finger into the fire. An ignorant man is bound to commit various lapses at different stages of life. Therefore, knowledge must necessarily be acquired. For that only the sages and seers always keep on imparting knowledge. Knowledge is also available in scriptures. This means that knowledge is always there. The knowledge by which Law of Eternity can be understood properly is also available in scriptures. Because we have distanced ourselves from that knowledge, we remain ignorant about the same but still we nurture the feeling that we know everything. This is also due to ignorance. Although doing *Adharma*, we claim due to misconception that we are doing Dharma. A child also at times says that he knows everything. But during examination, his teacher finds out his mistakes and therefore does not award full marks. The sages and seers impart knowledge on the Law of Eternity. But quite a few take interest in them. We are not even able to know what the Law of Eternity is although we owe our existence, sustenance etc. to it. The sages and seers want that everyone should understand this law and observe the same to attain bliss and freedom. To get some jobs, we have to acquire some qualification and undergo some training. That knowledge is only for our survival but that is not enough. The real knowledge enables us not only to maintain our bodies and live in the society peacefully but also to ultimately lead us to freedom. The Law about which we have discussed in the foregoing paragraph is also linked with knowledge.

Every person wants that he should protect his body, live in the society with peace and happiness, and ultimately attain freedom. In other words, he does not want to be subservient to anybody. He wants to be blissful. He shuns sufferings. He wants freedom from the shackles of rebirth and sufferings. He wants to be free from all bondages. He, who is inquisitive about this and makes efforts, shall ultimately attain bliss and freedom from sufferings, doubts, fear and desperation. By observing Dharma this state can be attained. This Dharma is the Eternal Dharma, i.e. the Law of Eternity.

Divya Darshan says, "To know the Law of Eternity is knowledge and to observe the same is Dharma. Dharma comes from knowledge and liberation comes from Dharma."

This is the process to attain self-realisation which brings with it bliss and freedom. All other knowledge, which is mainly for survival or living in society with status and position etc., is limited knowledge which would not carry us to our real goal.

Due to some knowledge and greater ignorance, we do a few things right, but we commit multiple lapses on a cumulative basis. Can we tell that we are on the path of righteousness and Dharma?

Right observance of Dharma would give us peace, bliss and ultimately freedom. It will take us forward on the path of self-development. If we are not able to achieve self-development, that means, we do not know what Dharma is and therefore we are not truly observing Dharma.

Many people try to appear as Dharmic persons by wearing special type of garments, performing different kinds of rituals, and wearing different patterns of sandalwood paste on their foreheads. But Dharma has nothing to do with the external coverings or make-ups. Divya Darshan says, "Knowing the Law of Eternity is knowledge; observance of the Law of Eternity is

Dharma." He, who appreciates and assimilates this, is on the path of divinity and ultimately he will attain divinity.

Therefore, you must know what Dharma is. Try to learn from him who knows more than you. You may learn from your brother, parents, teachers or from spiritual texts. You may also approach a Sadguru. It is also our Dharma to learn what Dharma is. So far whatever we have learnt, are from some Guru or other sources as discussed above. If we know everything, why do we commit mistakes? That means, there is inadequacy of knowledge in us. We should consider ourselves fortunate that we are increasing our level of knowledge by asking questions to others who know more than us and who are able to guide us. We should not feel ashamed to inquire from others. If we know one truth after another, that means, we are acquiring more knowledge. In this process if we proceed, one day we can realise the Supreme Truth, i.e. God or Brahman. Approaching a Sadguru and acquiring true knowledge is a special opportunity in this life. Then life becomes purposeful. That means knowledge takes us to greater heights, promotes us, and elevates us to infinity, immortality, eternity and unity. Then why feel shy to acquire knowledge from the sages and seers, from the knowledgeable and wise persons? Due to ignorance we shy away from admitting our faults or lapses. We are not able to tell the truth, however qualified or educated we may be. We think without falsehood we cannot manage ourselves. Rather we make all out efforts to hide the truth. But it is seen at times that an innocent man goes to the police station and unhesitatingly confesses to the crime committed by him.

Man has been gifted with a rare and fair form. Only man can elevate himself to Godhood. It is said that 84 lakhs of births he had taken before taking human form. He is still in a processing stage awaiting completeness. There are different grades of men. There are persons who behave like demons and some others behave like lower creatures. They are yet to reach their real manhood. They are in the making. In other words, evolution is still on. Therefore man should lead his life carefully. If he commits more sins, there is likelihood that he may be deprived of human birth in future and be demoted to the levels of lower creatures. Hence man should remain away from sins and always try to tread on the path of righteousness. It is like the game of Ludo. There are ladders and snakes in it. One can rise with the help of ladder. On the other hand, there are snakes ready to swallow and cause downfall. Every moment we are passing through virtues and vices. Therefore, we should consciously make efforts to increase our virtuous deeds. We should never allow ourselves to get downgraded to animal or sub-human categories. Our virtues shall propel us to higher and more qualitative births while sins shall push us to the cauldrons of sufferings. Scriptures describe five types of sacrifices (Pancha Yajna) which are –

- Bhuta Yajna- sacrifices for animals or lower creatures,
- Nru Yajna   - sacrifices for humans
- Pitru Yajna - sacrifices for ancestors
- Deva Yajna - sacrifices for Devas
- Jnana Yajna or Rishi Yajna or Brahman Yajna - Practice of True Knowledge.

Of all the above sacrifices, Jnana Yajna or Rishi Yajna is the best and highest form of Yajna that excels all other forms of sacrifices and gives eternal and unlimited result i.e. *Moksa* (Liberation or *Mukti*).

All religions guide mankind to peace and happiness. But people are not able to live in peace and happiness. Suffering is the rule rather than exception. Men clamour for peace but it becomes rarer. An angry man cannot get peace. A greedy man cannot get peace. In other words, unless one possesses divine qualities, peace shall be a far cry for him.

There is Law of Action. Whatever somebody does, the corresponding results also accrue to him. "Every action has got equal and opposite reaction," This Newtonian law of motion is also applicable to our own actions. If we undertake good actions, good results will ensue. If we do wrong things, the corresponding bad results will accrue and shall unfailingly come back to us. This Law of action is strictly enforced in the Law of Nature. Nobody can save us or give us any reprieve. We must be overly cautious while doing anything. The end result of sins is sufferings. Ignorance begets sins and sufferings; knowledge begets virtue and bliss. We are supposed to learn from our sufferings and refrain from sins. We must aim at increasing our virtues to get peace, happiness and ultimately freedom from all miseries.

Most of men are steeped in ignorance. They think that by taking shelter of any personal godhead, they can get rid of sufferings. But who is the dispenser of all fruits of actions? In the Shrimad Bhagavad-Gita, Lord Srikrishna says, "I am the dispenser of fruits. You have only the right to actions".

When the Supreme Power is the ultimate dispenser, how can any personal godhead deviate from the Law of Action and provide any relief or relaxation? So, everyone is bound to enjoy the fruits of his actions. Nobody else can intervene to dilute or manipulate the results. We should try to mend our ways and set right our actions so that we shall be happy with the ensuing good results. If we shall be repeating our lapses and approaching any powerful deity to forgive us, we would not be forgiven. In order to get rid of sufferings we are to find the right means for ourselves.

Many people do not believe in the existence of any such Supreme Power. Some other people believe in the Supreme Power, but they worship some deity of their own imagination. We are saddled with a host of desires. We pray God for fulfilment of our desires by performing different types of rituals and penances. The Gods created by our imaginations cannot protect us nor fulfil our desires. Because of this also, many people turn to become disbelievers. He is not God whom we imagine as such. The scriptures have tried to describe and give indication of Brahman in correct manner. Because we do not evince interest to know, we form our own ideas about God who is altogether different from Brahman described by the ancient scriptures as all-pervasive, all powerful and eternal existence. Gods of our imagination cannot give us anything since we only have created such Gods by our imagination. Whoever will try to know the Brahman as realised by the sages and seers, can attain everything, all peace and happiness, bliss and freedom. God cannot give us cooked food and remove our hunger. God has given us knowledge and intelligence by which we can utilise the available resources and prepare food for ourselves and for others. God is there in all of us as our knowledge, our intelligence, our strength, our seeing power and hearing power etc. We need not beg of Him anything else. He has provided everything. Nothing extra is to be created. By acquiring knowledge, we can know His scheme of things and get benefited. We are getting His blessings always and every moment. Due to cataract of ignorance, we are unable to understand Him.

      Sanatan Dharma

He is there as the Chit-Shakti or Conscious Energy. He is our intellect. He manifests as everything in this Creation. Without Him, we cannot exist.

God is Bliss-Absolute. He, who knows Him as such, realises Him. God is Freedom-Absolute. He, who knows Him as such, liberates himself. Whatever we require, God has already provided everything to us before we asked for the same. We are not aware of the same. Nor do we evince interest to know. We find it easy to create a God of our imagination and seek his help in every matter. We have been surviving even without knowing God. This means that God has made everything for our survival even before we asked for the same. We are able to function because of His power. We are utilising the knowledge that He has bestowed upon us. But man is not able to realise this. He also does not know how much he can be benefited by Him! He is not able to understand that God has provided milk in the mother's breast before a baby is born. Before creation of anything, God has made all arrangements for its working and maintenance. If man acquires enough knowledge, he can get so many things from God. God has given us so many things before we were born and before we asked for the same. We cannot even imagine what all He can give us! This means, if we know Him and thereafter ask for something, we shall get.

But what are we doing? We are forgetting God. In the process, we are delinked from God. How can we get rid of sufferings? The more a man knows Him, the more peace and happiness he would get. In other words, we can get rid of sufferings.

Even the disbelievers are better than those who worship an imagined God, expecting benefits from Him. The disbelievers reject any idea of God created out of human imagination. Therefore, they hastily conclude that there is no God. But that there is an Absolute God or Brahman who is different from the imaginary Gods is yet to be understood and accepted by them.

If somebody knows the greatness of God or role of God, slowly he would believe in the existence of God. God is Knowledge-Absolute. He manifests as the Creation although He is formless.

But man thinks it easy to perform some rituals more often followed with befitting celebrations in a joyful and exuberant manner to propitiate God and to get something in return. Hence the need for knowledge is not felt.

Lord Buddha preached four noble truths thus.

- There is suffering (Dukkha arising due to birth, old age, disease and death). This is the first truth.

- There is a cause for the origin of suffering. This is the second truth.

- The third truth is the cessation of suffering. That means, suffering which has come must also go once the cause of the same is known.

- There is a path to cessation of suffering. Once man knows and moves on this path, his sufferings shall come to an end.

In other words, we are to analyse the reasons of sufferings and take appropriate measures for cessation of sufferings. But, instead of doing this, we approach different deities of our imagination for alleviation of our sufferings.

We should know God's scheme of things and his laws. We should follow the Law to stay blessed. We should possess sattvic qualities and shun tamasic qualities. We should possess divine qualities and remain away from demoniac qualities. We should thus tread on virtuous path to get peace and bliss. Falsehood, crookedness, arrogance, jealousy and anger etc. would bring in more unrest than peace.

All divine qualities are there in the kingdom of nature. The Creation is sustained by means of divine qualities such as-

- Renunciation
- Restraint
- Spiritual Practice (Efforts)
- Service
- Truth
- Love
- Forgiveness

God has bestowed all these divine qualities upon everyone including animals. The Creation survives due to divine qualities. If a mother would not take care of her baby, the baby cannot survive. It is the mother who brings up the baby. The father takes care of the family. Even a tigress feeds its cubs and protects them. This shows that the entire Creation is sustained due to divine qualities.

He, who possesses these divine qualities, is really *dharmic.* Therefore, man's Dharma is to conduct himself on the path of righteousness with divine qualities for attaining self-realisation.

Truth is also an important trait that upholds the Creation. We expect others to speak truth. But we ourselves take to falsehood. We feel that one cannot survive by telling truth and therefore falsehood must be resorted to for survival. But if truth prevails everywhere at all points, then we all shall be benefited. We have survived due to truth. Without truth man's survival would be a big question mark. When somebody comes back home, his wife has kept food ready because she knows that her husband will return at a specified time. The wife expects her husband to tell truth. The husband also expects his wife to tell truth. We all expect our children to tell truth. A gang of robbers also obey and honour truth in their dealings otherwise the gang shall break away. They distribute their booties among themselves truthfully. Man is suffering because he does not know truth to the extent he should know. There would be disturbances in the family and in society if truth is not honoured and followed. Disaster and disturbances are bound to occur wherever there are deviations from truth. Many violate truth and ultimately go to courts for justice. Like this, in every phase of our life and even day to day living we observe truth because of which things happen smoothly and systematically. Similarly love and forgiveness are also two especially important divine qualities. Those, who possess love and forgiveness, are elevated human beings. Even the demons possess some divine qualities. They take care of their family and children. A demon king takes care of his kingdom.

If someone wants peace and bliss, God will not give any such thing separately. Unless man possesses or develops the quality of love in him, he cannot get peace and bliss. A jealous, crooked, or revengeful person cannot get peace and bliss. Bliss is an outcome of love. Bliss is something which is intangible and can only be experienced. If somebody serves others, many people will come forward to serve him. If somebody is of loving nature, all will love him; love shall come back to him from all sides. Divine qualities are God's gift which are there everywhere in the kingdom of nature. We should apply those qualities and conduct ourselves accordingly for peace and happiness of self and society. A person, who possesses great amount of material wealth, cannot satisfy everybody. But a person with divine quality of love can satisfy one and all. Love is intangible and inexhaustible. Such a man would be loved by millions of people. Love is therefore a great divine asset. If men and women understand the value of love and start loving each other, the earth shall become a heaven. Human beings can do this by upholding and applying the divine virtues which are the free gifts of God. They cost nothing. Service, love and forgiveness cannot be purchased by money. Money is exhaustible and transient whereas divine qualities are inexhaustible and permanent.

If some person possesses the quality of love, there would be manifold reciprocation of love, just unimaginable! God is there everywhere as love. His store house is here only. Due to ignorance we are not able to utilize the divine resources. The sages and seers utilized those resources and enjoyed divine bliss, eternal and unlimited.

God cannot mitigate our sufferings permanently. God cannot give us peace and happiness for all time to come. Let us therefore develop the divine virtues in ourselves. That is true Dharma and Dharma shall lead us to eternal freedom from all sins and sufferings, from the cycle of birth and death, and from the bondage of samsar.

TRUTH

Truth

Truth is a well-known word. Everyone knows truth to some extent and respects truth. In reality, this creation is full of truth. The beginning, middle and end of the creation are created, pervaded and regulated by truth. In other words, this creation is a manifestation of truth. Truth is indispensable not only for survival but also for getting peace and happiness in the society. Truth is the basis of life and vital energy. Therefore man cannot live for a moment without truth. He is himself made of truth. He vehemently reacts to wrong doings or falsehood.

Knowledge of truth is there in everyone. But that knowledge remains mostly in a dormant state. Once man evinces interest in knowing truth, the dormant knowledge shall get unfolded one by one. By dint of knowledge, one shall know truth. Knowing the truth is true knowledge. The more one knows truth, the more one lives in peace and happiness. Due to ignorance, the importance or greatness of truth remains unknown. As a result, at every step man gets beset with fear and doubt making his life miserable. "Ignorance is a great sin"- This is what the great Greek philosopher had exclaimed. Therefore truth must be known and realised in order to get rid of sorrows and sufferings.

Whatever has been discussed about truth in the foregoing paragraph is relative truth whereas the Absolute Truth is different from all these. The Absolute Truth has some intrinsic greatness in it. What is that Absolute Truth? What is the true nature of the Absolute Truth?

Truth is truth. Whatever is truth is truth only. The definition of truth is truth only. That which is called truth is nothing but existence which is realised as truth. Existence is truth. Whatever is truth is existence. Truth exists eternally. In other words truth is ever-present. Truth is not created. Truth cannot be destroyed. That means, truth is all-pervasive and indivisible whole present at all times, past, present and future. Truth is pure and unsullied. Truth is immutable, that is, without any *vikara*. It is not subject to decay, death or destruction. That is called Supreme Truth. When man realises this Truth, he gets bliss. There is neither any bliss nor sufferings at Supreme Truth. Nothing other than Supreme Truth remains. There can be no comparison to Supreme Truth. Therefore no simile or allegory is possible.

Truth can be explained by truth only. Because everything has been created and engineered by Him, everything has evolved from out of Him, no example can be cited to explain Him. While Supreme Truth is uncaused and unconditioned, He cannot be explained or realised through things caused and conditioned.

This creation is manifestation of truth only. As long as there is creation, there is *jiva*. Truth remains all along. Without truth, nothing would have existed.

Example

Jiva is truth and his gross body is also truth. The gross body is made of five elements which are also truth. The five elements have come from some other truth. Like this when we analyse truth layer after layer, whatever remains ultimately is the Supreme Truth.

The subtle body is also truth. There is some causal factor behind its creation. That is causal body. This causal body also has come from some other truth. Like this if we proceed, we shall reach Supreme Truth from where everything is manifested.

Water is truth. Bubbles come out of water and again merge in it. It is also a truth. Water possesses certain properties. It is also a truth. If we proceed in this way from cause to the cause of cause, we shall reach a causeless cause which is the Supreme Truth.

Water is a combination of Oxygen and Hydrogen. It is a truth. Oxygen and Hydrogen have come from some other truth. If we proceed in this way we reach a causeless state which is Supreme Truth or the supra-causal state.

To elucidate further a few examples can be cited.

Without wood or fuel, the fire can't manifest itself in its gross form. Had there been no fire, there would not have been any splinters. Had there been no water, there would not have been any ice, not even the bubbles. It is clear from the above that there is some basis behind the creation of each and everything. The essence or the ultimate sub-stratum of everything is the Supreme Truth which projects or upholds everything.

In this creation of living and non-living, sentient and insentient things it is the Supreme Truth which has been playing

His eternal game. His play is so mysterious that it is not easily comprehended by the men of ordinary knowledge. Only a *jnani* (wise person) can unveil the mystery. His ability to realise the Supreme Truth is also bestowed upon him by the Supreme Truth. Everything in this creation is 'Truth' only. Whatever we see or perceive such as forms and qualities, the gross and the subtle are all manifestations of Truth. Whatsoever have occurred in the past, whatsoever are occurring at present and whatsoever are going to occur in future are all manifestations of Truth. Whatever is occurring, whatever is occurring but not being perceived are all manifestations of truth. The 'time' is also truth. The measuring system such as hour, minute and second are all truth. Whatsoever have happened and not happened are all truth. Living and dying are as true as birth. All actions within the span of birth and death are truth. In whatever ways one talks, sees, laughs, makes others laugh, cries, makes others cry, plans and contemplates are all truth. Similarly, why someone has taken birth and why he died are all governed by truth. One lives in happiness while another suffers. How and why happiness or unhappiness is there are all caused and conditioned by truth. To understand truth, to misunderstand truth and not being able to understand truth are also truth.

Fear, shyness, anger, greed and infatuation etc. are all truth. Why all these have appeared and how they influence us are also truth. To tell the truth is truth. To tell a lie is also truth. The effects and side-effects of this are also truth. To prove falsehood or to assert that it is not a truth but falsehood, truth is needed. In other words, truth can prove falsehood but by falsehood, truth cannot be proved. This is also a truth. By truth alone both truth and falsehood can be established or proved. There is no other way out except truth. It is clear from the above discussion that truth expresses itself both as truth and falsehood irrespective of person, place, time and environment.

Distortion of truth is termed as falsehood. Falsehood is only a modified version of truth. In other words, if things happen in a way other than the way it should have happened, it is termed as unfair or unjust, untruth or falsehood.

To attain the ultimate goal of liberation, some law is to be necessarily observed or some Dharma is to be performed. Observance of the Eternal Law is Dharma. Any deviation from Dharma is known as *adharma*.

In this creation everything is truth. Divya Darshan explains the Truth by classifying the manifestation of truth in four categories.

Temporal Truth, Partial Truth, Causal Truth and Supreme Truth

Temporal Truth: Time is like an ever-flowing stream. It is dynamic. It moves on. At different times objects take various different forms. They exist for a limited time and then pass away. Those are time-based or temporal truths. Lightning, rain and bubbles etc. come and go. A plant grows to maturity, bears flowers and fruits, decays and dies. Many events happen in the womb of time. Those are truths for a particular period. We come across various truths at different times. They vanish thereafter. Something or other happens every moment. But those are temporary phenomena. Whatever occurs or whatever events take place, are all true for that time period. A close observation will reveal that things change at every moment. In other words, they become different the next moment. Events happen on a non-stop basis one after another and things keep on changing although imperceptibly. It is the incessant process of change that makes different things appears at different times. Some are noticed but many things go unnoticed. The chain of events never breaks. The process of change goes on eternally. We ourselves are the products of that process. Changes do take place in us and around us in a ceaseless manner. Birth itself is a change. So is death. All these happenings are temporal or time-based. These are called time-based truths or temporal truth.

Partial Truth: When there is temporal truth, there exists definitely some basis of it. Temporal truth is only a link in a chain. Many other links forego and many other links follow for change is a beginningless and endless chain. In other words, temporal truths that appear have not come out of nothing. Just as rain presupposes cloud and water vapour, ice or bubble presupposes water, diurnal brightness presupposes the Sun, volcanic eruption presupposes some semi-liquid and gaseous matters, earthquake presupposes earth, plant kingdom presupposes mineral kingdom. Similarly a temporal object which appears and disappears has also backward and forward linkages. Temporal truth cannot be a causeless entity. There is definitely some basis of the temporal truth. That is known as Partial Truth. Five basic elements such as ether, air, fire, water and earth; five *tanmatras* such as - sound, touch, form, taste and smell and eleven sense organs (five sense organs, five organs of action and mind) come under Partial Truth. From these five basic elements such as - ether, air, fire, water and earth, the gross world is created. So is the gross body. From the five subtle elements (*tanmatras*), the subtle body is created. These are not visible. When the gross world, gross body and gross matters are destroyed (including the plants and animals) they all merge in the five gross elements. Likewise, the subtle body that is made up of the subtle elements also get dissolved into the subtle elements. Wherever there is a form (*rupa*), there is trait (*guna*). Wherever there is *guna* there is *rupa*. This means both *rupa* and *guna* are destructible. Hence they come under partial truth.

Causal truth: When there is partial truth, there definitely exists a cause of it which is also a truth. This is known as causal truth. This is 'Om'. The entire creation has come out from this state. This state manifests as three qualities such as- Sattva, Rajas and Tamas. A, U, M (called 'Om') represent the three qualities such as- Sattva, Rajas and Tamas. These three qualities are also known as *trishakti* namely, Brahma, Vishnu and Maheswar. The creator of the universe is Brahma, the preserver is Vishnu and the destroyer (who causes mutation or transformation) is Maheswar, the Lord of deluge. 'Om' represents the truth Absolute who is the cause of generation, operation and destruction. He pervades the entire creation as *Sat, Chit* and *Anand. Sat* means that which exists eternally, i.e. irrespective of past, present and future. *Chit* means consciousness or knowledge. *Anand* (bliss) means peace and happiness, experience of which makes every cell exuberate, exhilarate and expand. It is not just a mundane pleasure. It is an extraordinary and unique experience which the realised sages attain. This *sat* (existence) expresses itself as *Chit* which means consciousness or knowledge. By virtue of knowledge when Truth is realised Bliss is experienced. There is nothing else but Bliss. Causal Truth cannot be explained in words. It is to be experienced only.

Supreme Truth: Since *Anand* (Bliss) is qualified has also an end. Since it is linked with *guna*, it is supported by some other existence. That basic sub-stratum is transcendental state. This is

Supreme Truth. This is named differently such as – God, Atman, Brahman etc. The Supreme truth has no beginning, no end too. He is ever present. Everything is created due to His greatness. He is changeless. He is immutable. He is without any form or quality. Hence He is beyond creation or destruction. When He is realised, supreme bliss dawns upon the realiser. From the Supreme Truth, everything else is manifested. That is why He cannot be explained by example or simile. He is unique. There is none like Him. He is the supra-causal factor. He is both the material cause and efficient cause of everything, every subject and object, every effect and every event. He is the essence pervading the evanescent universe. Nothing in this universe can reach Him, gauge Him and even guess Him. Thoughts cannot reach Him since all thoughts emanate from Him. Words cannot describe Him. Intellect cannot comprehend Him. Thought, intellect and words are but His manifestations of the Supreme Truth.

Realising the Supreme Truth and the mystery of the Creation Jagadguru Sankaracharya asserted with unwavering conviction, "Brahman is Truth, Jagat is false." That means- Brahman is, Jagat is not. Many other sages in Vedic and Upanishadic ages also proclaimed and preached this Supreme Truth. Rishi Yajnavalkya while explaining the Supreme Truth remained silent after pronouncing "Neti Neti" which means, "not this, not like this." The Supreme Truth who is none other than the Pure Consciousness (Prajnanam Brahman) willed to express Himself through multiplicity. Hence He manifested as the Creation.

The temporal truth, partial truth and the causal truth are all pervaded by the Supreme Truth. The temporal truth gets dissolved in the partial truth. The partial truth gets dissolved in the causal truth. All these three categories are subject to change but the Supreme Truth (supra-causal) exists eternally, without beginning and without end. It is uncaused and unconditioned, hence supra-causal. It is Self-Consciousness which is changeless infinite existence beyond any sorrows and sufferings.

This Truth has to be realised in order to get rid of sufferings. On realising the omnipotency and omnipresence of Brahman, the sages said, "After knowing which nothing remains to be known, after attaining which nothing remains to be achieved, He is Brahman and everyone should meditate on Him". On knowing that Truth, all doubts, all fears and all sufferings vanish and true self is realised.

Divya Darshan preaches that everyone should be in constant quest for the Supreme Truth so as to know and to be. On realising the Supreme Truth one can cross the ocean of samsar which is full of sufferings.

"Oh mankind! Forgetting your True Self and mistaking this stage for your abode and unreal role for your 'Self', how long will you continue to be tortured in the frying cauldron of lust and greed, pride and prejudice? Arise; enkindle the flame of awareness within. Get ready to return to your peaceful, immortal and heavenly abode and get back your Eternal, True and Pure Self. Then only you will free yourself from all miseries and fear. Remember! **You are the immortal and emancipated soul.**"

— Sadguru Sri Sri Arjun

KNOWLEDGE

Knowledge

True devotion comes after acquiring knowledge. By preliminary knowledge, we come to know something about God. Thereafter we believe in His existence. If we know still more, we can learn about His Greatness. Thereafter, we shall have devotion. From knowledge, comes *Bhava*. The devotion, which is an offshoot of *Bhava*, is the real devotion.

Thereafter by His Grace *Mahabhava* dawns upon the spiritual aspirant. True Love is an outcome of *Mahabhava*. Union is the outcome of True Love. That is the state (stateless state) when the individuality gets merged in that Supreme Self. Is it possible to transcend to this Supreme State without knowledge?

Although man does not know what devotion is, he sometimes considers himself to be a devotee. According to the Bhagavad Gita, desireless *Bhakti* is true *Bhakti*. If we wish to gain something in exchange of *bhakti*, that is not real *Bhakti*. As long as the desireless *bhakti* does not overwhelm the devotee, he cannot realize God.

How such desireless Bhakti will come? As long as man does not acquire true knowledge, desireless *Bhakti* will not come. Desireless and unconditional love will not come without true knowledge. Desireless action is possible only after acquiring true knowledge. It means desirelessness is an outcome of true knowledge. By knowledge only one can discriminate what is desireless and what is not. Without knowledge, nothing is possible.

The children say, "There is God". The grown-ups say, "There is God." The seers say, "There is God."

There is difference in these assertions. The seer alone knows and thereafter he makes the statements. The child does not know yet he also makes the statement. In other words, there is gradation of knowledge, which is quite evident from the assertions made by three categories of persons.

Due to gradations of knowledge (Ranging from total ignorance to perfect knowledge) different persons perceive a particular thing in different manners. Standpoints are different. Viewpoints are different. The angles of vision are different. That is why different ideas and expressions are observed. Due to ignorance only, many people claim themselves to be atheists.

The education we receive now-a-days helps us earn our livelihood only. By this knowledge, we just manage to survive or take care of our bodies. At times, the present education is inadequate as a result of which we are not able to earn peace and happiness in our society. Our mind wants peace. Our intellect wants happiness but the knowledge that is instrumental in earning for us the much desired peace and happiness, is not being pursued by us. Our conscience seeks freedom but we are not evincing interest in that knowledge which can really bring us freedom. Remaining at the mental level, we make wishful thinking for getting liberation. At the mental plane, liberation is impossible. So, one has to move from mind to intellect and from intellect to conscience. One has to reach the plane of *Mahabhava*. At that state only, one can attain God.

The knowledge we possess and the so-called virtues we have acquired are not real knowledge, not also real virtues. According to scriptures, there is no question of worship or devotion in the plane of Supreme Truth. It is a state of Unity. It is a stateless state bereft of classifications or divisions. It is only a limitless and homogeneous Unity called Pure-Consciousness or Self-Consciousness which does not admit of a second entity anywhere and anytime. It is an Infinite Existence. It is eternal. It is Omniscient, Omnipotent and Omnipresent.

Whatever we express about Brahman through speech is not Brahman. Speech cannot express Him. It is He only who is the cause of speech. Brahman is not an outcome of any mental process. Rather mind's functions are caused and conditioned by Him. He is present everywhere. He is not confined to any particular idol or ideology. He is not confined to a particular person or place. He is not confined to a specific time or any particular temple. He is all-pervasive. He is Omnipotent, Omnipresent and Omniscient. He is present even in stones and pillars. He is in you. He is in me too. This visible gross universe is only His one-fourth part. The subtle state is three-fourth. We do not know even the gross universe fully and properly. The remaining three-fourth is subtle and invisible. All the four parts are to be known to know the Brahman. Due to lack of full understanding, some devotees stake various types of claims. Some devotees say that their Vishnu is great while some others contend that their Shiva is great. This is only a subject matter of first step only (i.e. one-fourth of the total).

Brahma, Vishnu and Maheshwar who are the creator, sustainer and destroyer respectively are related to the visible gross universe as the processes of creation, preservation and destruction pertain only to the gross universe. There are no such happenings in the subtle world.

At the time of great deluge, Brahma, Vishnu, Maheshwar, the Sun, the Moon and the stars etc. will also get dissolved in the Supreme Truth. The Supreme Truth is the *Turiya* state which transcends all other three states such as waking, dreaming and sleeping.

Different religious camps enter into conflicts among themselves in their efforts to establish their own Gods. Divya Darshan does not speak of any particular religious belief or dogma. Divya Darshan preaches the Law of Eternity, which was there even before the Creation. Human beings, their divisions and sub-divisions into various religious followings are only subsequent developments.

Some devotees pray the formless God. Some others advance justification for worshipping different personal Godheads with forms. But according to Divya Darshan, "He, who knows Him in forms and also without forms, knows Him better". Hence true knowledge has to be acquired. Knowledge is our life. By knowledge alone truth can be unravelled and we will have faith, devotion and love for truth. Without acquiring knowledge of truth, we carry mistaken conviction that we possess devotion and love for God.

Lord Jesus had preached the true concept of love. But people do not have sufficient understanding of love. Had they really understood what love is, this world would not have been torn by discord and internal dissension leading to darkness.

Love is a misunderstood term. If someone likes a good singer or if someone likes a beautiful appearance, we cannot call it love. In other words, merely liking some qualities or appearances is not Love. Love transcends all names, forms and qualities. Love is unconditional self- surrender. It is linked with Atman.

We have got six enemies within. They are - desire, anger, greed, attachment, ego and jealousy. Infatuation is more often than not mistaken for love. The union between self and self is true love. But due to ignorance or absence of self-knowledge one is not able to understand and appreciate the essence of love.

Knowledge is light. Ignorance is darkness. Divya Darshan therefore lays emphasis on knowledge and advises to face light rather than darkness. By means of knowledge, one can know the self. By knowledge, one can know the world and by knowledge, one can know God.

According to Divya Darshan, the meaning of Dharma is, knowing one's true self. With this end in view, whatever is performed is Dharma. When we have forgotten our true self and we do not try to know it, then how can we claim that we are observing Dharma! Whatever we are doing, are directed towards our survival or at best for a comfortable living. But by this, Dharma is not observed in totality. It is incomplete and distorted because we are not aware of the ultimate goal of life.

Divya Darshan raises a few fundamental questions.

- Why do you take food? The answer is- for survival
- Why do you want to survive? Answer- for peace and happiness.
- Why peace and happiness?

Many will falter and fumble at this stage. Divya Darshan explains that everyone seeks peace and happiness because that is every one's true nature. Although we have forgotten our true nature, we instinctively try to regain the lost paradise. Upanishads say- "The Atman is Bliss-Absolute." That means bliss is our true nature. Only for attaining bliss, we take food, we want to survive, we maintain our bodies and we also try to live in a society with peace and happiness. In other words, the very purpose of human birth is to attain peace and bliss. But it never occurs to us that all our actions are unknowingly but instinctively directed towards realising our true self.

When we will know what is our goal or destination, all our actions will be streamlined and we will move faster towards our goal. In other words, our journey towards the goal will be shorter. But due to ignorance, we are waylaid. We go here and there through by-lanes instead of highway. This highway is Dharma which leads us to the destination i.e. self-realisation. Without the aim of self-realisation, whatever we do in the name of Dharma, is a wasteful endeavour only. Whatever little we gain from out of the occasional observance of Dharma is also squandered in course of our aimless wanderings and purposeless pursuits.

But those, who sincerely aim at self-realisation, shall definitely attain the same before long. On the other hand, by aimless pursuits, we shall get sufferings only. This is not the only birth we have taken. We had taken innumerable births before. We have enjoyed a lot. We have suffered a lot. But still, our thirst for sensual pleasures remains. Human form is the best form. It is possible to reach the destination in this life. But being oblivious of the noble purpose of our birth, we try to seek pleasure in the varieties of ephemeral objects just to satisfy our ever-increasing desires that capture us like an octopus.

If we are not able to rid ourselves of the desires and lust for sensual pleasures in this birth, then in which birth shall we renounce the sensual pleasures and try for self-realisation? Self-realisation is the aim of human life. It is high time that we discriminate between good and bad, permanent and transitory. Before it is too late, we must try to gain self-knowledge.

The first lesson of spiritual knowledge is- "There is God"

The second lesson is- "God has created everything. He resides in everything."

The third lesson is "Thou art that." When we are not even aware of the first lesson how shall we realise God? How shall we realise the teachings of Vedas and Upanishads? There are four *Mahavakyas* which are as under:

"Thou art that."

"I am verily the Brahman."

"This Atman is Brahman".

"Pure Consciousness is Brahman."

To realise the essence of all these four *Mahavakyas,* one has to acquire knowledge. Knowing the Truth is knowledge. God exists as Supreme Truth. Hence Divya Darshan does not ascribe any form to God.

How does God exist?

God manifests himself as different truths in different things. For example, hydrogen and oxygen, when combined, become water.

This is a truth. The proportion in which the compound should be prepared is also a truth. Hydrogen is a truth. The other component i.e. oxygen is also a truth. Everything is a manifested form of God. The more one knows the truth, the more he can utilise it and be benefited. God manifests Himself everywhere as forms, qualities, and knowledge. But in absence of true knowledge we are not able to realise Him. God exists everywhere as Truth. When we fall asleep, we do not know whether and when we shall wake up. We lose body consciousness. We become unaware of everything. When we are asleep, who wakes us up? When we are asleep, we also breathe and remain alive. Who makes it possible when we are ourselves not conscious of the same? Which power helps in getting our food digested? This is a very common feature, which occurs in every one alike. Does this not indicate the presence of a benevolent power that always takes care of us?

God remains everywhere and in everything as truth. Suppose we want to cook rice. To do this, we take the help of some truths, such as, water, fuel, rice, time and the quantities thereof. Unless all these truths are known and applied properly, rice cannot be cooked. That means the more we know truths, the more we are benefited. Without trying to know truths, we simply utter the name of God. Simply by uttering name of God, God will not provide us cooked rice. Truth cannot be known without knowledge. Hence the basic requirement is knowledge. Without learning alphabet, we cannot read any book. Likewise, knowledge is the basis of truth. How shall we cognize truth as truth without the help of knowledge. Hence, Divya Darshan says, "There is nothing as falsehood or untruth. Not realising truth is falsehood. Not realising truth is ignorance. Not realising truth is darkness. There is nothing separate as darkness. It is absence of light. It is a particular situation created by light itself. The people generally say that there is darkness. People also say that there is light. Likewise, there is something called truth. There is also something called falsehood.

According to Divya Darshan absence of light is darkness. When one is unable to realise truth one says, 'it is false'. In other words, when one fails to realise the basis or background of existence, he says it is non-existent. That means, when truth remains undiscovered many untruths crop up. That is how we take the shelter of falsehood. In reality truth is all-pervasive. God Himself manifests as truth. The more one acquires knowledge, the more one knows the truths and the Brahman who is none other than the Supreme Truth. God is Bliss Absolute. He who realises this true nature of God shall get more and more bliss. Bliss is different from worldly pleasures. Worldly pleasures are transitory and followed by sufferings but God is ever blissful. God's bliss is inexhaustible. Hence, God is the basis of eternal peace and bliss. He who realises God enjoys pure bliss perennially. Therefore in order to get peace and happiness, God-realisation has to be aimed at. Wherever there are fear, doubt and despair there are miseries. Opposite to these is pure Bliss, which means freedom from all sorrows and sufferings.

There is truth in everything. God only manifests as truths through some eternal principles, which are called Law of Eternity (*Sanatan Dharma*). The operation of this Law of Eternity brings in its course 'changes' and consequently truths. In other words, the Law of Eternity expresses itself as various truths.

The Law of Eternity is God's words or God's Laws. For everything, there are underlying laws. Man wants to live. For this there are some laws or principles. If those are not followed, man's living gets disturbed. There are also certain principles for getting peace and happiness. For living in a society also some principles are to be followed. Peace is not any material object. It is something to be realised from within.

The Law of Eternity is also in operation in the nature's kingdom. For birth, there are certain laws. For death also, there are certain laws. For bondage, there are laws. For liberation, there are laws. Both for growth and decay, the Law of Eternity is in operation, as the term indicates, eternally. This Law was there before the creation. This Law shall remain in future also. This Law shall take us to our destination from where we started our journey.

Divya Darshan says, "Knowing the Law of Eternity is knowledge and observing the same is Dharma. Any one, who observes the law, is entitled to peace and bliss. In God's kingdom, everything is for peace and bliss. But due to ignorance, peace and bliss remain a far cry.

Divya Darshan imparts true knowledge by explaining the greatness of Sanatan Dharma to the people. Divya Darshan never approves any blind following. Divya Darshan reasons out and rationalises things and preaches simple techniques for proper observance of the Law of Eternity. Divya Darshan, in its well-integrated approach, teaches mankind why and how to survive, how to live in society and how to get liberation.

The law of nature is that after birth there is an instinct to survive and thereafter to live in peace and happiness. Ultimately we have to strive for liberation. But whatever knowledge we have acquired is only for leading an ordinary life. Even some persons do not bother to acquire knowledge, which would help them live in the society in peace and happiness. In absence of that knowledge, they are not able to adjust themselves in a society resulting in internal distrusts and disturbances.

The sages have charted out many paths for God-realisation. But in course of time, the teachings have been diluted. Many superstitions have come in, as a result of which there are lot of confusions which act as impediments to God- realisation. Divya Darshan presents to mankind a very clear path to self-realisation.

Theory of Change or Transformation

Change is the eternal law of eternal application and not an occasional exception. Change is the inherent property of everything, be it visible or invisible. Change is the dharma, the truth of the universe. Things keep on changing every moment and get transformed into other forms. The latent qualities and also the physical organization of every unit of existence undergo change every moment. Everything is therefore dynamic whether living or non-living. Beyond this dynamic existence there exists another all-pervasive transcendental state, which is neither dynamic nor static. That is why that supreme state is called inexpressible. Sometimes that state is said to be static, sometimes dynamic. That state is also known to be both static and dynamic. Further that state is said to be static containing within it all powers to commission the dynamic process. But when viewed as an indivisible whole, no such qualities or qualifications can be attributed to that supreme state. He is therefore neither static nor dynamic. He is beyond, hence inexpressible. All the manifestations are changeable. All manifestations are but self-expressions of the Absolute Existence, which is changeless and eternal.

We come across varieties because of the ever-operative phenomenon of change or transformation. In other words, varieties are the products of a continuous self-propelled process of change, which occurs eternally giving birth to newer and newer creations every moment to make the creation lovely and lively, colourful and complete. In this process of change, things come and go, appear and disappear not for nothingness but to reappear with more meaningful purposes and deliberate designs in various permutations and combinations, although those are unitary in essence.

This process of change or transformation was existent in the past, is in operation now and shall continue in future also. This process of change is therefore ever existent. This process brings about creation and destruction of various forms and qualities. The whole creation, of which we are a part, is a product of this grand process of change.

Only after perceiving a certain thing we say- 'I am seeing, it is happening, it is there etc.' In fact what we have perceived and experienced is a the-then state or position of the matter. We don't see the same thing next moment in its exact state or condition because the contents and the patterns have undergone changes in the meanwhile in an imperceptible manner. When we do not see something which we had seen or experienced earlier we say it was earlier there but now it is not. It has been destroyed. It has vanished. It means that creation, preservation and destruction go on every moment on a non-stop basis and very fast caused by an eternal principle or Law known as the Law of Eternity.

As a result, we find consistencies and co-ordination in the natural phenomena around us and even in our internal systems.

But the process of change in some cases is very slow as a result of which we fail to cognize the process. The creation we see around us, the environment that envelops us, have all taken innumerable years to evolve up to this stage.

It is difficult to study and comprehend the vastness and multi-dimensional nature of the process of change, which occurs both in positive and negative ways, and also in all possible directions. In a split second, changes do occur which are beyond our perception capacity. Lightning appears and disappears at once. In a split second, an atom bomb explodes. Light travels at a speed of three lakh kilometres a second. We have never seen the sunlight. Only when the same is reflected on the objects and when the reflected rays fall on our eyes then only we say that we have seen the sun light. Likewise, changes occur in the universe unbelievably fast, which is beyond our perception capacity.

Magnet attracts iron. The movement of iron is visible but the force that acts upon iron remains unseen. Wind blows from high pressure to low pressure areas. Movement of the wind is not visible. But when the trees are swept away, when the leaves flutter, when houses are raged to the ground creating cracking sounds, at that time we say that there is a cyclone. We usually say that the sun rises in the east and sets in the west. The rising sun here is the setting sun elsewhere. The setting sun here is also the rising sun somewhere else. In fact the sun never rises nor sets. We experience the changes due to rotation and revolution of the earth we live in.

Again whether there is light or darkness we can cognize only by some other light i.e. the light in our eyes. We cannot see that light in our eyes even though it enables us to see everything. The sky appears blue. The rope appears like a snake. The parallel rails look as if they are united at a distance. What we call a plain surface will be seen to be undulated if examined with the help of a microscope. An ordinary glass or crystal appears like a piece of diamond. Thus so many deceptive appearances keep on puzzling our mind.

It is only the white colour that creates the spectrum of seven colours and makes this creation appear colourful. In the process of change or modification some colours are absorbed and some colours are reflected.

Be it the process of photosynthesis, or blood circulation system, be it the respiratory system or digestive system, be it the solar system or an atomic structure, everything is a product of change and therefore contains within it the process of change. In other words, the process itself is the creator, sustainer and destroyer of everything that we come across.

Our coming across variety of objects and even all our imaginations thereof are but parts of that process of change. All sorts of transformations of energy become possible only due to the ever-existent process of change. Changes do occur every moment. During this process, we come across various forms and qualities. We come across ourselves too. We are all products of a complex process of change. Change takes place within us and around us continuously. Things appear to exist because change has made them so. Someone writes or speaks. Someone listens or observes. Someone introspects or contemplates. These activities become possible because of the underlying process of change.

It would not have been possible to read, had there been no change. The generation of ideas and imaginations is also a change. An idea fading into oblivion is also a change. Remembering and forgetting are also results of change. We move the pen to write one letter after another, words after words. Here also the process of change is very much involved. Changelessness is a state when everything will come to a standstill position i.e. without any motion or vibration, without any flow or flutter. In absence of change, our lips would not move, our jaws would not move, tongue would remain tied, muscle would remain tight, eyelids would not wink, eyeballs would not slide and as a result, we would be speechless and motionless as statues. The planets would not move in their orbits. Day and night would not be possible, as there would not be any rotation of the planets. Seasonal changes would not be possible, as there would not be any revolution of earth. There would be no sun, no earth. Light would lose its speed. Air would be motionless. The Sun is nothing but a mass of burning hydrogen gas. Every moment, fresh hydrogen gushes into the burning process and it goes on like that. In other words, the sun is also a product of change. The entire universe is a product of change. The process of change is a self-propelled mechanism. It is all-embracing. It changes everything but the theory of change remains unchanged. That is the Law of Eternity.

Everything comes into being only because there is an incessant self-generated process of change. The aboriginal man would have been taken aback when his cottage was swept away by an invisible gush of wind. When a sudden fire in the jungle had burnt his belongings to ashes, he must have fled away with awe and harboured in his mind a barrage of unsolved questions. When he had seen for the first time a dark patch of cloud tarnishing the clear blue canopy of heaven, he would have stared at the same, misconstruing it for an ominous sign. Thereafter a torrential shower would have drenched him and his belongings. With the change of seasons, while experiencing biting cold in the wintry night, he would not have found any answer to the cause of his shivering. The scorching rays of the summer sun must have parched him. He would have frantically tried to find out who had been creating all such mischief for him. He would have been disappointed not being able to see the invisible hands behind all such happenings. After sunset, he would have experienced darkness. He would have probably felt as if he had lost his eyesight. Further, once a tender child, he became a vibrant youth and now he is old and weak with his limbs emaciated. When he would have seen a dead body for the first time, he would have wondered how the consciousness stealthily passed away for some unknown destination leaving the body still and stale. He must have pondered over but failed to trace out the reasons for such changes triggering the process of creation, preservation and destruction.

The sages say that He, who has created all these forms and qualities, is named as Brahma. After the creation, the created things remain for some time. The sustaining power is called Vishnu. In other words, Vishnu is the preserver or protector. For example, a tree remains as a tree for a certain period. Man survives from birth to death. For his survival, he requires many essential things like air, water, food etc. He, who arranges and organises all these, is called Vishnu. Every created object, plant or human being is subjected to an end called death. Trees wither away. All living things die out. He who causes this process of death is known as Maheshwar. In other words, creation, preservation, and destruction are possible because of three Godheads, namely Brahma, Vishnu and Maheshwar respectively.

Who has created all these? Who is sustaining all these? The answer comes, "Ishwar (Lord) is doing all these". Different religions admit of such powers, which are named differently. Generally He is known as God. The term God can be expanded as Generation, Operation and Destruction (G-O-D). Matter is transformed into energy. Energy is transformed into matter. Various forms of matters are created through a process of chain reactions according to different properties latent in different matters and their inherent combining capacities, resulting in innumerable physical and chemical changes, further creating new substances, new properties, new effects, new environments, new actions and new reactions, ever changing in a continuous process of evolution to continuously create products with new patterns and new designs, new arrangements and new organisations. Thus every moment a renewed universe or a better universe comes into being. This dynamism shall cease when a realiser attains final equilibrium.

Three important aspects of change are creation, preservation and destruction. Without change how can there be creation? How can there be preservation? How can there be destruction? Whether change is an effect? If so, what may be the causal factor behind the change? In other words, whether change is self-propelled or impelled by some other driving background force? If change is caused, what is its cause? Who is causing it?

 SANATAN DHARMA

It is a well-known fact that matter becomes energy and energy becomes matter. But a question still remains to be answered. Whom does this power of causing such transformations belong to? Whether the power is inherent in matter? Whether the power is inherent in energy? Who initiates the process of change and what for? Who directs, organises, or regulates the process of change? It is not easy to find a solution. Various religions ascribe this causal factor to another power called GOD and not to matter or energy. It is to be admitted that there is a background power behind the process of change in course of which different products appear before us. We ourselves are also products of such a process. Without that causal power, all these effects would not have been possible.

Sadguru Sri Sri Arjun emphatically affirms the existence of an independent and omnipotent entity. According to him, He who causes the process of change Himself remains unchanged. In other words, He is a changeless entity but is the sole governor of all changes. It is our first and foremost duty to know Him since He is responsible for our appearance, sustenance and destruction in this creation. The creation, in turn, owes its origin to Him.

The scientific man perceives the changes. He comes into being through the process of change. He enjoys the changes. He is afflicted by the changes. He passes away. It is a change. Even after he passes away, the process of change continues unabated just as the process was continuing before he was born.

But unfortunately, man does not want to know the eternal maker of all these eternal changes. If he could witness the ceaseless process of change in and around himself, probably he could have unravelled the mystery of the creation and solved many unsolved questions. If he would deeply contemplate on the process of change, his faith on the existence of a supreme power would be strengthened. He would have strong conviction on the great powers and potency of the supreme power. The more a man is ignorant of this process of change, the more he would be subjected to sufferings and be afflicted by the effects of change.

Divya Darshan therefore focuses on the process of change so that man can tide over the effects of changes by acquiring knowledge on the changeable phenomena. This is the surest way to peace and happiness. The moment he starts his enquiry into the process of change, he would start getting peace and happiness. A time will come when he would perfectly understand the process of change. At that time, God's Greatness will no longer remain for him a matter of round-eyed wonder or a question mark. Rather a pure and uncontaminated sense of love towards God will dawn upon Him. He will be thoroughly engrossed in that superb thought and realise the goodness of God and attain the blissful state to get ultimately immerged with Him.

Process of Change: Its greatness and significance

- If there is any strong proof for God's existence, it is the process of change. Had there been no change there would have been neither this creation nor we; the question of realisation, freedom or bondage would not have arisen. The creation, our realisation and we - all these are but the products of that grand process of change. The process of change gives rise to various forms and qualities. Without this process, there would have been neither forms nor qualities.

 SANATAN DHARMA

- Due to the process of change, it becomes possible for all of us to march onward from ignorance to knowledge ultimately to know the invisible supreme power that remains unchanged as the substratum of the process of change. We name that invisible power as God, Ishwar etc.

- The process of change gradually leads all of us to our origin.

- Various experiences are also the effects of this process of change.

- His Lila or play takes place through the process of change. His play only makes us realise His significance and greatness.

Atman is characterised by changelessness. Atman is Self. Whatever appears to change can be, for the purpose of understanding, categorised as non-self (*Apara*). The latter is nothing but the inherent qualities or power of the former. In reality, self-consciousness is all-pervasive. There is nothing outside the kingdom of self. There is nothing other than the self. The self and the so-called non-self are one and the same. All changes are therefore apparent and not real when viewed from transcendental aspect. The process of change, which appears real, is a lower truth that leads us to the Supreme Truth i.e. the changeless eternal self-consciousness. Ultimately, all apparent imbalances, imperfections and disequilibriums disappear and it is only a homogeneous, all pervasive pure consciousness or perfect equilibrium which remains and reigns supreme in complete silence blissfully and eternally.

Who is the cause of all becomings?

It is the bounden duty of everyone to know Him who is the essence of everything. On realising the great power that is the source of all powers, the *rishis* have named Him as *Brahman, Atman, Ishwar* etc. That highest state is realised by knowledge power which is *Chitshakti*. While explaining the true self or Brahman, it is normally said that He is neither *Chit* nor *Achit*. He is neither existence nor non-existence. He is that inexpressible unmanifest consciousness by whom we know *chit*, by whom we know *achit*, existence and non-existence. He who can realise that becomes that. He realises, "I am Brahman; I am Atman; I am the witness consciousness; I am in every one and everyone is in me; My play goes on incessantly; I am the pure consciousness who does not admit of any decay, death or bondage; I am the Knowledge Absolute."

This is called self-knowledge, Knowledge of Brahman or the total knowledge, eternal and undivided.

Law Of Karma (Action) & Reflection Theory

(Reflection theory is a concept to explain the whys of all happenings. It is said that as you sow, so you reap. It shows how one's own actions return either to reward the doer or punish.)

Fruits of actions unfailingly follow actions. Gross action yields result. So also subtle action. For example, when we try to know about God, it is an action. As a result, we come to know something about God. Bad deeds, bad thoughts give rise to bad results. Due to ignorance, we are unable to know this truth. Result is complementary to Karma just as Newton's third law; "Every action has equal and opposite reaction."

In this Creation, there is heaven. There is hell too. Wherever there is peace and bliss that is heaven. Where there are sufferings, it is hell. Our mental actions or reactions activate our sense organs and also the organs of action and finally corresponding actions take place. According to scriptures, we perform karma but God awards results. Divya Darshan says that the results come from the kingdom of nature. If a picture is kept in front of a mirror, that picture gets reflected on the mirror. This also happens in the kingdom of nature.

Water will drench us. Fire will burn us. These are properties of water and fire or laws of nature. No fruit accrues if there is no karma. When there is no karma, God also cannot give any fruit. If He gives, there will be violation of the Law of Eternity. Without performing appropriate karma, we ask God for desired results. How can we get? When we obey His laws and perform appropriate karma, then only we shall get the desired results. There are mainly two types of karma. (a) Action with desire (b) Desire-less action. The results are different. It is certain that good action shall yield good result. By acquiring more and more knowledge, man can comprehend karma properly. He can also understand how the fruits of action are reaped.

Reflection Theory is another significant subject of Divya Darshan. It is an important tool to understand the mystery of the Creation. The law of Karma and Reflection Theory are very much inter-linked. Reflection is not an independent function. Before reflection something else has to happen in order to cause reflection. This means, reflection is an effect. The cause and effect are different. Every moment different incidents take place in different places. Reflection happens thereafter. Reflections differ as incidents differ. Reflection gives hint or indication about the already happened incident. Incident also gives indication about the reflection that is going to take place. Whatever happens is an incident. It is a change. The resultant is reflection. Since change is involved in the process, it is necessary to understand 'change'. We are not able to perceive the Law that effects the change. After change is effected, we call the resultant as creation. Brahman willed, "I shall be many". The unqualified Brahman by His Will became qualified. That means by His omni-potency, He became tri-qualities such as Sattva, Rajas and Tamas. Tri-qualities, three in one, are also known as the primordial energy which is unmanifest when the three are in the same proportion or in a balanced state. When this static equilibrium gets disturbed, creation takes place. First comes *Mahatattva* and thereafter comes *Ahankar. Ahankar* creates separateness and identifies oneself with particular form or quality. Mahatattva is also known as Buddhitattva. Subsequent to *Ahankar, comes* mind, five tanmatras, sense organs and five elements. Within the ambit of the aforesaid tri-qualities, all other forms and qualities are manifested. These forms and qualities create illusory effects. 'Om' expressed itself as the personal God-heads. There is knowledge in Karma. The reflection theory is applicable to karma.

God expresses Himself as Truth as well as reflections. If we scold others, we shall be paid back in our own coins. Man yearns for peace and happiness. Therefore he has to observe those truths which are necessary for getting him peace and happiness. For getting peace and happiness it is essential to possess qualities like humility and love. He who knows this secret, can captivate the whole world. A sweet tongue is an effective tool to win over others. Love begets love. *Bhakti* brings blessings. *Shraddhaa* brings good wishes. Divya Darshan lays emphasis on goodness such as good thoughts, good deeds and good conduct. In other words, divine qualities shall definitely bring us peace, happiness and freedom. By possessing divine qualities, one will get blessings and ultimately realise God. This is the surest path to God-realisation.

Acquiring goodness amounts to attaining God. Therefore one should enquire what is good. Good appearance, good quality, good knowledge, good energy, piety, beauty, perfection, justice and truth come under the purview of goodness. It means, what is divine is good. God is good. God is unity, infinity and eternity. Therefore, all spiritual efforts should be directed towards acquiring true knowledge and divine qualities which shall culminate in *moksa* or liberation.

God is *Sat-Chit-Anand*. We call Him '*Sat*' after realising Him by '*Chit*'. Because that existence is there, we call Him '*Sat*' by '*Chit*'. This means He is neither '*Sat*' nor '*Chit*'. *Chit* is Bliss-Absolute. After realising '*Chit*', comes Bliss. He is therefore different from *Anand* (Bliss) also. He is beyond bliss. He is '*Neti Neti*'. He is also called '*Parambrahman*'. That Existence called *Parambrahman* is His unmanifest state. He manifests as *Chit shakti*. By '*Chit*', He is realised. He is neither '*Sat*' nor '*Asat*'. He is neither '*Chit*' nor '*Achit*'. He is '*Neti Neti*'. That supreme state cannot be explained by words. Only a true realiser knows who He is.

Why do we suffer?

The answer would be – due to our ignorance.

Next question would be – what is ignorance and how to dispel it? If we do not know about ignorance, then how can we get rid of it?

Ignorance is not complete absence of knowledge. It is incomplete or distorted knowledge. It has a semblance of knowledge. Ignorance is not opposite to knowledge although ordinarily it is understood to be so. Ignorance represents lower truths whereas knowledge represents higher truths. It is a well-known fact that there is a gradation of knowledge. As and when we acquire more and more knowledge, ignorance simultaneously fades away just as darkness goes away with the lighting of a candle. Ignorance is the cause of sufferings. Knowledge relieves us from sufferings. Knowledge leads to peace and happiness. Perfect knowledge leads to perfect bliss. That by which we perceive or cognize or understand or experience anything is called knowledge. By knowledge we understand things and make others understand. When we explain certain things to others and when others understand the same, we say that they have learnt or understood. That means, whatever we have already learnt is knowledge. What we are going to learn is knowledge and that which we make others understand is also knowledge. Therefore knowing, explaining or teaching come under the category of knowing, that is knowledge.

True nature of Knowledge

Is there anybody who expresses him by himself? Is there anybody who regulates him by himself? Is there anybody who identifies him by himself?

He is an inexpressible existence who has neither any beginning nor an end. He is ever present. He, by whom everything else comes into being or in other words He by whom everything else is caused and conditioned is the Supreme Being. He manifests Himself in innumerable ways. In other words, He makes Himself known in various ways, i.e. in various forms and qualities. He regulates Himself as and when required.

He knows everything. He who knows everything can also do everything. He who can do everything is no doubt omnipotent. He is omniscient. The *Vedas* describe Him as most powerful. He, who is omnipotent, can make everything possible. Therefore, He is conscious energy. True self is pure consciousness. The *Vedas* call him Consciousness-Absolute *(Prajnanam Brahman)*. By this *Chit Shakti* or Conscious Energy, everything becomes possible and by that Conscious Energy everything can be known. This knowing power is known as knowledge. There is absolutely no difference between chit and knowledge although usages are differently made. Consciousness causes everything. When by using consciousness something is understood or explained, it is called knowledge. These two words such as consciousness and knowledge essentially denote the same thing. The consciousness manifests as knowledge.

From the gross to the subtle and the subtle-most Brahman, the entire knowledge is divided into two parts for easy understanding. Those are *apara* and *para*. *Apara* connotes the lower state while *para* stands for the higher state of knowledge. Broadly speaking *apara* relates to the perceivable or material existence (becomings) whereas the *para* knowledge relates to the Being by whom everything else is caused and conditioned.

Knowledge, as expressed in this Creation

The creation is an integration of various forms and qualities. The forms are visible but the qualities are not. The qualities are perceived or experienced by means of knowledge. We gather knowledge of various descriptions such as - whether the form is ugly or beautiful, black or white, long or short? We also try to perceive the qualities of the objects.

Different individuals put in their varying grades of knowledge at different places and at different times. Whatever the man contemplates now, were there in different shapes and sizes. Now after seeing those objects once again, man is experiencing or recollecting that knowledge. To elucidate further, let us take the example of a rose plant. After recognizing its various parts such as leaves, flowers and thorns, we call it a rose plant. Likewise we differentiate varieties of roses according to their colours, breeds etc. Let us take the case of all other things in this creation. After knowing various qualities, shapes and sizes of some matters, plants or animals, we call them by different names. Knowledge enables us do so. Knowledge is involved in all these. It can be said that whatever knowledge we acquire on a particular thing earlier existed in some form or quality. In other words, knowledge is involved in whatever we see or experience in this creation. That means, the true nature of everything in this creation is knowledge. The creation is the manifestation of *Brahman*. Brahman is Knowledge Absolute.

Past impulses and knowledge

Everyone is born with some past impulses. A person, in whom the predominant quality is *Tamas*, possesses least knowledge. The person, in whom the predominant quality is *Rajas*, is called *Rajas*ic and the person in whom the predominant quality is *sattva* is called *sattvic*. Similarly those in whom we see predominance of animal instincts are called beasts or animals. Likewise, a human being is called so because his mind is developed and he is capable of contemplating on different subjects. Those in whom, divine qualities are predominant are known to be *devas*.

Gunas are the modifications of knowledge. In other words, the latent knowledge expresses or manifests as *Gunas*.

Different names are attributed to different things on cognizing the qualities present in them. In different forms corresponding qualities are expressed. Different qualities also evolve as different forms.

In other words, the characteristics of a dog have taken the shape of a dog. Human qualities have taken human form. Each and every being advances through different course and in the process it acquires some impulses in an evolutionary process.

Although the qualities correspond to the forms taken, all the inner qualities are not always expressed. Those come to light in specific situations and environments. During the course of our life, whatever one sees, hears, thinks and reads are stored inside him as knowledge. This knowledge which remains in latent form is recollected after seeing, reading, listening or remembering. This is called *samskar* or the impulses.

The great Greek philosopher Socrates had thrown light on this aspect. According to him, "You have taken many births. Knowledge acquired in several births is stored in you. Lot of powers acquired in several births are conserved in you. Because the qualities correspond to the forms you have taken, that much knowledge as required by the form only gets activated. All that knowledge acquired by you in the past is very much there inside you. That is not at all wasted. You have only forgotten that."

Socrates has further explained as follows- When somebody tells us something we nod our head in approval. How do we approve or disapprove? The reason is whatever we have heard are all inside us. When the knowledge stored inside match with the fresh inputs we say, 'yes' or nod in approval. When there is a mismatch, we nod in disagreement.

Suppose we were planning to go to the market for purchasing something. At times we forget to do so, being occupied with other works. When someone speaks about the market or the related topics, we at once remember that we are also to buy something. Many such examples can be cited. Like that, by seeing, listening and recollecting, many such thoughts lying in our subconscious mind gets stirred and buoy up to the surface. Thus we remember forgotten things.

If you see somebody making or designing something you are also able to do that. How could you do that? It means you might have made such things earlier. Now when you come across that design you are able to understand the knowledge behind that design and put the same into practice by recollecting that knowledge from within. There may be initially some imperfections in your doings but slowly new ideas and new skills develop in you by which you improve upon till you are perfect or near perfect. When something is perfectly done, it is to be understood that your complete knowledge has been recollected. Acquiring some knowledge means developing your own latent knowledge. There are also people who cannot understand even after seeing a process of work. It may be due to the fact that he had learnt that many years back or many births back. Or, may be, he has taken only a few human births.

Knowledge-Shakti Absolute

The great scientist Archimedes had said, "Give me a small platform outside the earth. I can move the earth even." This appeared surprising and unachievable. The secret was that he had developed the lever theory by which a heavy mass could be displaced.

By dint of knowledge man could know the latent powers of different kinds of matters, molecules and atoms. He could know how they could be put into different uses. For example fire is a combination of light and heat energy which can be put into several uses. Again after knowing that the same fire can be extinguished by carbon dioxide, he is able to get rid of fire. Similarly there are different types of diseases and remedies. The more he acquires knowledge, the more he can enjoy. With the advancement of science, varieties of techniques have been developed to offer mankind comforts, peace and happiness by their proper use. It is but the knowledge, which is the remote control of all remote controls.

Each of the divine qualities such as renunciation, self-restraint, spiritual practice, service, truth, love and forgiveness, is a divine power. The scriptures describe about the super natural powers demonstrated by the demons. All these powers are acquired by knowledge. If somebody is hostile to us, we can win him over by love. If somebody differs with us we know what type of methods to be applied to win over him. If someone possesses a cruel heart, we find out some psychological ways to soften his heart. This is also done with the help of knowledge. In other words everything is accomplished by proper application of knowledge. It must be remembered that knowledge is power and without it everything is meaningless. One must understand the strength and significance of knowledge so that one shall thirst for knowledge. By acquiring knowledge a man can very well distinguish himself in the society. The knowledgeable man is really powerful. Only a powerful man can serve others. He becomes a guiding light for the society. He can enjoy freedom. He can be fearless. He alone deserves supreme bliss. He can know the past present and future also. For him nothing remains unachievable. It is evident that knowledge provides strength. Knowledge is truly the Power Absolute or the Energy Absolute by which all other powers and energies can be controlled and utilized.

Energy and Matter

Energy is invisible and indescribable. Energy manifests as matter. Matter is a form of energy. Here the energy is the body and all its constituents. There the energy takes the forms of mountains, oceans and different objects of the phenomenal world. The invisible energy becomes the matter after several stages of modifications. Matter is also transformed into energy. Thus matter and energy are one and the same. In other words, there is a unity or homogeneity in heterogeneity. There is nothing other than energy. Total energy is constant, neither increasing nor decreasing. Changes like deaths and births are merely intermediary phases. Through changes only new products are created and the creation wears new look every day with new colours.

Divya Darshan explains this by its "Theory of Change" according to which there exists an unchangeable conscious entity that governs all changes. It is not the matter which has got the power to transform itself into invisible and indescribable energy.

It is not the energy that has got any power to transform itself into meaningful and significant world of matters. A conscious force is definitely at the background of everything i.e. creation, operation and destruction. A systematic Law is undoubtedly at work to maintain the consistency, regularity and universality.

Man is himself a product of this grand cyclic process of change. Changes do occur within and without every moment everywhere. The objects change. The subjects change Therefore the mutual relationships also undergo change calling for adjustment or resetting always. Changes are multi-dimensional. Changes take place in the gross as well as the subtle worlds simultaneously. We, who are composed of varieties and variables, live in a world of varieties and variables, interact with them to create momentary equilibriums and dis-equilibriums until a state of permanent equilibrium is reached which is a perfect state of Bliss or the heavenly abode.

Triguna

Chit shakti (consciousness energy) by its inherent greatness manifests itself as three qualities such as *Sattva, Rajas* and *Tamas*. They are the basic three qualities. These three qualities form the basic ingredients of the creation. Due to varying proportions of the three qualities, various other qualities are created in various permutations and combinations, which subsequently manifest as forms. In other words, these basic three qualities are begetters of all forms of different colours, shapes and sizes. These three qualities are the organizers, arrangers and the promoters of all qualities. These three qualities are known as primordial power of the eternal nature. These three qualities represent three great powers, which are known as will, knowledge and action. This classification, in a broad sense, is nothing but different states of knowledge. To put it in a different language, the primordial trio of *sattva, Rajas* and *Tamas* unfold themselves in various ways wielding three powers such as will power, knowledge power and action, which can be broadly termed as knowledge. Knowledge is the true nature of the three qualities. This trio as discussed earlier undergoes various modifications by three powers such as will power, knowledge power and action to unfold itself as this universe. This universe also radiates knowledge.

Ignorance and Maya

One of the characteristic features of these three qualities (*Sattva, Rajas* and *Tamas*) is that in some places there appears more knowledge and somewhere less knowledge. Viewed from a layman's angle, the living being clearly demonstrates more knowledge than the non-living. The *jiva* does possess some knowledge on each and everything that appears in between matter and the highest Brahman. He possesses some knowledge, which is limited. With limited knowledge he cannot know things fully. Each and everything in this creation is different from the other. Each is a different form or state. One form cannot understand the other form. It is particularly so because the lower form cannot comprehend the higher form. This 'not-understanding' or 'not-knowing' is ignorance. Ignorance does not mean absence of knowledge. It means inadequate knowledge. Due to ignorance, a *jiva* mistakes a particular thing as some other thing. For example a rope is mistaken for a snake. Due to ignorance, essential things are overlooked but things of lesser importance or value are attached priorities. Ignorance generates pride and prejudice.

   SANATAN DHARMA

Due to ignorance poison is regarded as nectar. As a result, *jiva* suffers from doubts and despair, agonies and anxieties, fear and frustrations. All these varieties of effects are nothing but mental illusions or *Maya*. It is said that man suffers due to *Maya*. Trying to explain this mysterious concept of *Maya*, the sages say that *Maya* is existent and also *Maya* is non-existent. Then they also say *Maya* is neither existent nor non-existent.

For example, when we say there is *Dharma*, we can't simultaneously say that there is no *Dharma*. Likewise when we say that there is truth, we can't say at the same time that there is no truth. But simultaneously saying that *Maya* exists and *Maya* does not exist, does not make any sense to the common man. The question is- Whether Maya exists or does not exist? But such a statement cannot just be ignored as meaningless. It is neither existent nor non-existent. It is positive; it is negative; it is neither positive nor negative. Such types of statements although quite significant are nevertheless meaningless for the common man. However the statements are quite meaningful in the sense that *Maya* exists for the ignorant whereas it does not exist for the wise or seers of truth.

He, who is established in wisdom, becomes one with the being. For him *Maya* is neither existent nor non-existent. But when *jiva* is not able to understand *Maya*, he is caught in the cobweb of *Maya*. *Maya* is nothing but the play of the three qualities or *Triguna*. *Maya* has got two powers, i.e. Projection power and Veiling power.

By projection power varieties are manifested. In other words, multiplicity becomes apparent. By the veiling power, the *jiva* is shrouded by ignorance and forgets its true self. As a result of that, he suffers. *Maya* cannot be pointed out as this or that. No symptom can be ascribed to *Maya* for a proper diagnosis. It exists; it does not exist. Both the statements are true. It remains with the ignorant, does not remain with the *jnani* (realiser). To put it in another way, knowing only limited or relative truth is *Maya*. Knowing the Absolute Truth, amounts to cessation of *Maya*.

Where there is knowledge there is no *Maya*. Everything looks crystal clear once you have perfect knowledge. Therefore the *jnani* remains a witness. In a higher sense, except the realised souls all others have some degree of ignorance. Therefore every one suffers by the play of *Maya*. It is ignorance of Truth that creates illusory effects. It is knowledge of Truth that leads us to Unity. Absence or inadequacy of the knowledge creates multiplicity or plurality.

The effects of ignorance are such that one cannot know oneself as ignorant. Rather one considers oneself to be more knowledgeable than others. Not being able to know one's own ignorance is also ignorance. Due to hypnotising effects of *Maya*, it will not occur to an ignorant person that higher and still higher knowledge remains to be known. The day he decides in his mind to learn more, his progress starts.

Greatness of knowledge

- Knowledge is life; knowledge is the vital energy. Without knowledge, man is lifeless.

- The more one is knowledgeable, the more he is lively and vivacious.

- By the help of knowledge the *jiva* is able to do everything.

 SANATAN DHARMA

- By knowledge, man realises all truths and benefits out of them.

- By knowledge, man can realise God and enjoy supreme bliss

- Knowledge gives courage, patience, inspiration and fearlessness

- By knowledge, man can know past present and future.

- By knowledge, man discriminates between good, bad and enjoys divinities.

- By knowledge, we measure and evaluate everything. Without knowledge everything is meaningless/ valueless.

- By knowledge man gets rid of sufferings

- God is knowledge Absolute. Hence it is said, "Prajnanam Brahman". Brahman is pure knowledge or Pure Consciousness. He who surrenders to knowledge surrenders to Brahman.

- Knowledge is light. Where there is knowledge, there is no darkness of ignorance.

- By knowledge, man earns virtues. By ignorance he commits sin.

- Due to varying level of knowledge, we differentiate things such as matter, man, insect, animal and God etc.

- Knowledge is power. He, who possesses knowledge becomes powerful. He becomes Knowledge-Absolute.

- Knowledge protects all of us. All our resources are protected by knowledge.

The conscious existence manifests itself as various forms and qualities. In the process, the basic sub-stratum i.e. consciousness manifests itself as Sun, Moon, stars, planets and all other living and non-living objects which after completing the cycle again merge with that basic substratum.

The process is going on incessantly, ages after ages. Upanishads in this context say, everything is created from Brahman and ultimately is merged with the Brahman. To be created, to exist undergoing natural modifications and ultimately to merge with Him, there are some laws or regulatory process. Creation, operation and destruction are all regulated by this Law. During the course of operation of this law or during the working of the process, we come across varieties, which include *jiva*, Ishwar and Brahman. Everything is a manifestation of Brahman but due to ignorance the *jiva* is not in a position to know this mysterious working and significance of Sanatan *Dharma*, the Law of Eternity. That is why he is not able to observe *Dharma*. He does Ad*harma* (opposite of Dharma) as a result of which he suffers. In order to tide over all sorts of sufferings it is essential for everyone to know the Law of Eternity and surrender to the Almighty with a pure heart.

Without knowledge, it is not possible to know Him. By knowledge everything can be understood. Every human being must endeavour to regain his lost paradise by recollecting the forgotten knowledge. That is why Divya Darshan lays utmost emphasis on knowledge. *Dharma* emanates from Knowledge and liberation from *Dharma*.

"This is no life at all. To know the infuser of life is true life. Cast off ignorance, acquire true knowledge and develop divine qualities."

DIVINE QUALITIES

Divine Qualities

[Divya Darshan gives lot of importance to the seven divine virtues. If one can practice even one of these virtues he will enjoy bliss. The below mentioned article is a synthesis of various talks on the divine virtues delivered by Sadguru Sri Sri Arjun at various places and times. It is not an exact translation of his talks but a gist.]

The Law of Eternity is divine and it works on the principles of divine qualities. The seven divine qualities (Renunciation, Restraint, Spiritual Practice, Service, Truth, Love and forgiveness) are very much present in all living beings whether they know or not. The seven divine virtues form the underlying basis for this Creation which is unfolded layer after layer from the causal to the subtle and from the subtle to the gross by the Law of Eternity which is none other than the Sanatan Dharma. This Law of Eternity emanating from the causal state manifests itself as the seven divine qualities in the subtle Creation and thereafter in the gross Creation of names and forms.

Divya Darshan lays great emphasis on knowledge and divine virtues for effective spiritual practice that leads the aspirant to the spiritual goal. With intense inquisitiveness, a spiritual seeker starts his spiritual practice and keeps on acquiring true knowledge. He also tries to inculcate divine virtues in him. Reading, listening, meditating and contemplating are the ways to acquiring knowledge. The spiritual seeker divinises himself by instinctively expressing divine qualities in his conduct. In course of acquisition of knowledge, he unveils one truth after another and purifies himself.

The entire universe owes its existence to the divine qualities. Divine qualities bring peace and happiness to life. The opposite of divine qualities are the demoniac qualities. With demoniac qualities, none can be happy. On the other hand, divine qualities are inexhaustible i.e. without any limitation or erosion. The Creation is lively and vibrant only due to divine qualities. Divine qualities bring fulfilment to life i.e. attainment of the divine goal. The secret of observance of the Law of Eternity lies in the divine qualities. He, who spontaneously conducts himself with the divine qualities, is pious and he truly observes Dharma that leads him to the goal of self-realisation.

What does the spiritual mendicant gain from the spiritual practice? The answer is- 'Divine Virtues' that pave the way clear to attainment of the goal of self-realisation. He comes to know the greatness of God and His role play. He becomes keen to know and observe the Law of Eternity. Thus, he observes Dharma and realises the Supreme Truth. The Creation is a manifestation of the divine qualities. Therefore, all the divine qualities are discreetly present in and around us. When divine qualities or virtues become our way of life, we lead a divine life which is full of happiness, peace and bliss. Divya Darshan explains the importance and indispensability of the divine qualities for a happy and harmonious living and urges upon everyone to practise the seven divine virtues. They are- Renunciation, Restraint, Spiritual Practice, Service, Truth, Love and Forgiveness. Those are explained briefly in the following pages.

"Whatever religion or sect you may belong to, liberation is impossible without self-knowledge."

— Sadguru Sri Sri Arjun

RENUNCIATION

Although this quality comes first, all the divine qualities are interlinked with each other. This quality is especially important because by this quality, the jiva has come from Brahman and again by this quality, he will be merged with Brahman thus completing the grand cycle. This is such a great power that all apparently impossible things can be made possible by it. Without this quality of renunciation, the system would not have been dynamic. We cannot think of a motionless Creation characterized by inertia only. No evolution would have taken place. There would have been no Creation even. Tendency of renunciation is there in every being in this Creation. Due to this tendency, a person is able to move on the path of self-development even though this tendency is not perceptible to the outside world. All scriptures in the world have therefore given importance to this divine quality of renunciation. It is true that lot of benefits accrue to the people who possess the quality of renunciation or the spirit of sacrifice. By possessing this quality man gets release from the snares of illusion. Without this quality man's progress would have halted. Due to the grace of God, man has taken birth on this earth with this great quality of renunciation. Man is lucky to have this great divine quality but due to ignorance man is not able to understand the importance of renunciation and that is why he has been suffering a lot. Had he not possessed this quality of renunciation, he would have got more sufferings; his survival would have been impossible. There are many examples of great persons who have sacrificed a lot for others. The sages have also sacrificed their comfort for the sake of God. Lord Buddha had sacrificed his family and kingdom in quest of truth. When the question of renunciation comes, people are usually afraid. They fear that if they will sacrifice everything, how will they survive? This feeling comes due to ignorance. If one thinks deeply, one will know that his survival has been possible due to this essential divine quality of renunciation. Our journey starts from renunciation and ends up with renunciation. Man moves on the path of life's journey due to this divine quality. Man is really a great renunciate. He finally relinquishes everything for the sake of others.

If someone wants to go to a particular place, he starts walking. He is to lift one step after another. One foot is to leave the ground first; thereafter the second foot will also leave the ground and move forward. In other words, one has to leave the present spot to move to next spot. That means, without renunciation or sacrifice, progress is not possible. Similarly, a child must leave the mother's lap or his play kits to go to school for education. Take for example a scientist who has made so much sacrifice to invent or discover certain things for the benefit of the world. He sacrifices all his comforts, forgets about his food, and even puts his life at risk for accomplishing his task. That is why God has probably gifted man with inquisitiveness.

But the ignorant men do not realise the importance of sacrifice. For them, the truth remains veiled. Even the ferocious animals like the tigers make lot of sacrifices for their cubs and bring them up with lot of care. That means sacrifice is a natural quality in all beings. A mother bird, starting from laying of eggs to hatching and thereafter feeding and protecting its little ones makes a lot of sacrifice. Wherefrom do they learn to make such sacrifice? Throughout the kingdom of nature the principle of sacrifice can be seen. That means sacrifice is a God given quality. There are umpteen examples of people sacrificing their lives even for the sake of their kin or kingdom, for race or religion, for truth and love. Those, who realise the value of sacrifice and make selfless sacrifices win the hearts of millions and become immortal. Divya Darshan says, "Sacrifice does not bring sufferings, rather it brings happiness, bliss and divinity."

We have taken birth due to sacrifice; we go ahead on the path of self-development to ultimately reach our goal of self-realisation due to sacrifice. Man starts discarding one thing after another from his very childhood. A time comes when this world has to be renounced. Body, mind, intellect and even the Creation are to be renounced. A time comes when nothing remains to be renounced. This state is called the Supreme state. Rishi Yajnavalkya while explaining about Brahman remained silent after pronouncing 'Neti Neti' which means, 'Not this, not like this'. After renouncing everything, realisation of self is possible. Only renouncing the house property, family and children is not adequate for this purpose. Those who are at the lower level of knowledge cannot understand the true import of renunciation. One must know what all have been renounced and what else are to be renounced. Finally, renunciation has to be renounced. Then only one can move to the highest state. A spiritual seeker has to think in this line and then only he can reach the highest state. He, who realises the importance of renunciation, can advance faster.

The sages had renounced everything and that is how they could reach the Supreme state. It is to be well understood that a renouncer finally attains everything after which nothing remains to be achieved. One must possess the necessary quality or qualification before possessing big things. Entertaining worldly thoughts, one cannot enjoy the Supreme Bliss which is possible only by renunciation. Some leave the worldly life and go to jungle. But while remaining in the jungle also they may get obsessed with the worldly thoughts. Then what type of renunciation is this?

The scriptures instruct mankind to give up desires. He, who follows it, can develop himself faster and attain self-realisation. For a true renouncer, what is there to lose? Hence there is no question of any loss and consequent suffering. By this quality of renunciation, a spiritual seeker can transcend the lower truths one after another to finally reach the Supreme state.

By renunciation, self-development is possible. Renunciation brings peace and bliss. Life begins from renunciation and ends up with renunciation. Renunciation frees one from all bondages and consequent sufferings. Renunciation uplifts one to the Supreme state where nothing remains to be received, nothing remains to be renounced.

We all have been sacrificing something or other in our personal lives. Parents sacrifice so many things for the children. People will be motivated to sacrifice if they understand that they are going to get better things. Since people do not have idea about the higher aspects of life, they cling to the smaller things considering them as indispensable.

At the highest level, it will be well understood that nothing is renounced. Only there is a change in thoughts or perceptions.

Lord Buddha said, "Craving is the cause of sufferings". The common people are unable to understand or appreciate the import of this statement. Some people argue, "Whether desire for liberation is not a desire?"

The sages clarify that desire for liberation is no desire. It is one's instinct to know the Self. Whatever is done for realisation of Self is Dharma. Desire for sensuous enjoyment is desire that is the cause of sins and sufferings. That way, God-realisation is not possible.

Due to ignorance, people sacrifice certain things in exchange for something considered to be more gainful. But desireless renunciation is true renunciation that can bring infinite peace and bliss. Spiritual bliss is free from anxiety and fear. Those who are attached to worldly matters cannot attain self-realisation. It is to be remembered that renunciation is the Law of nature.

Renunciation does not mean giving up or running away from the samsar. It means living in this world but with a different understanding, with a different vision. Renunciation is practiced at every step. Any movement involves renunciation. Any change involves renunciation. Any renunciation involves a process of sacrifice on one side and acceptance on the other side. The jiva after leaving his Supreme state has been born as jiva. Again by renouncing only, he will go back to True Self which is the Supreme state. In other words, by renunciation only he will be able to attain liberation. He has to renounce everything other than his True Self. He has to go beyond his body, senses, mind, and intellect. He has to renounce the samsar in order to realise his True Self. He has to renounce the non-self to realise the Self. Anything other than the Self is non-self. (But the reality is that, there is nothing other than the Self. Everything is Self only). When Self is realised everything becomes Self. Everything vanishes except Self. Ishavasya Upanishad says- "The Almighty pervades everywhere. Everything belongs to Him. Whatever is available to us are all for our use. But we are not the owners. Only the Almighty is the owner. We can be dispossessed of everything whenever he chooses to do so. Hence it should always be remembered that all the possessions ignorantly claimed to be ours are not really ours. Everything belongs to Him." Once the seeker realises this truth, it is said that he has truly renounced. This feeling is renunciation. In other words, it is a state of knowledge which does not involve physically forsaking anything. We breathe in because we also breathe out. We have left our childhood. We attained youth. We have to leave our youth and become old. This is the law of nature. Renunciation is the law of nature. This law is also applicable to the vegetable kingdom as well as mineral kingdom. The fruit leaves the mother tree to develop into another tree. The electrons keep on moving and join with others to form new substances. The root works day and night not just for itself but also to nourish the whole tree. Every part of the plant is engaged in a predetermined manner helping each other for sustenance. Renunciation does not mean only rejection. It also means acceptance. It means abandoning something for the sake of some other. We, as human beings, are bestowed with inquisitiveness. We must keep on reviewing our existing knowledge. We should give up our obsolete knowledge to learn newer and newer truths. Lower truths must be abandoned for the sake of higher truths. Lower goals must be relinquished for the sake of the highest goal. That only can lead us to real evolution. Low-value

 SANATAN DHARMA

items must be given up for things of higher value. Our mind-set must change. Our vision must change. We must analyse which is permanent and which is not. We must hold on to the eternal and renounce the ephemeral things we come across on our way.

SELF-RESTRAINT

Life cannot run smoothly without self-restraint. Self-restraint helps one proceed fast towards the goal. Just as a motor vehicle cannot run faster in absence of a proper brake system, similarly life journey gets obstructed and retarded if there is no self-restraint. There is an intimate relation between renunciation and self-restraint. Self-restraint is the outcome of renunciation. That means, one has to renounce certain things to have self-restraint. Renunciation also comes on practising self-restraint. That is why we find that a true renunciate is a restrained person.

Self-restraint means controlling power. Man possesses this quality from his very birth, as it is a God given quality or a divine quality. Those, who are under the clutches of their sense organs, cannot restrain themselves. That is why they suffer a lot. At times, man loses control over his sense organs resulting in lot of disturbances. As a result, many sufferings in the forms of disease, accidents, clashes and mental unrest etc. raise their ugly hoods which distract him from moving towards his goal. The wise persons understand this well. But the ignorant cannot think of the indispensability of self-restraint.

Man is endowed with lot of powers within him. In appropriate situations, these dormant powers rise and become clearly perceptible. For example, during phases of sufferings, a person struggles and many creative qualities in him come up. He may get more and more devoted towards God. His tolerance capacity may increase. But due to want of self-restraint, man's hidden qualities cannot blossom up. When a man talks more, not only he wastes his energy, but he tells many exaggerated things and even lies. He may, in order to impress others, be pretentious; as a result of which people in course of time reject him as a liar even when he speaks some truth. If a man sleeps excessively, he becomes lazy and useless. Rather he suffers from more diseases. If a man eats excessively, he becomes indisposed and suffers. As a result, he suffers physically and mentally also. Quarrels occur between individuals and groups because of lack of self-restraint. God has bestowed upon us lot of powers. It is our responsibility to conserve the same and utilise properly. That is why, even though we are strong intrinsically, we behave at times like weak creatures. Birds and animals are also seen to maintain self-restraint and discipline. They instinctively follow the natural laws perhaps more than the human beings. Self-restraint is also seen everywhere in the kingdom of nature. The sages are so powerful because they possess the divine quality of self-restraint.

Restraint helps a spiritual mendicant to move faster on the path of self-development. It must be remembered that without self-restraint, renunciation is not possible, and without renunciation, self-restraint is not possible. Both are divine qualities, and they are intertwined. Self-restraint brings balance to life. A person becomes more stable by the quality of self-restraint because of which he becomes stronger physically and mentally. Internal power gets strengthened by self-restraint. Self-restraint enables one to acquire more and more power. Self-restraint not only protects us, it also helps us attain our goal. A restrained man is a successful man.

Restraint or self-discipline is always observed in nature. The various ingredients of air always maintain their limitations and proportions. The oceans confine themselves to their shores. The fire remains sheathed everywhere until a particular situation is created to make it appear as a devouring flame. Every matter reacts in a manner consistent with its latent properties, which are pre-designed. Slowly but systematically, a seed evolves into a plant. The earth and all other planets move in a predetermined way in their orbits.

 SANATAN DHARMA

SPIRITUAL PRACTICE (SADHANA)

Self-restraint is essential to do spiritual practice properly. There is an intimate link between self-restraint and spiritual practice. Man cannot live without work. He is always engaged in some work or other, mental or physical, be it good or bad. According to the Law of Action, he reaps appropriate results thereof. Due to ignorance, man is very often unable to distinguish between good and bad. This brings sufferings to him. Karma is undertaken with the purpose of living a good life with peace and happiness. But that does not happen. It is due to ignorance about right action. Due to ignorance, he thinks that he has come to this world only to enjoy. He usually prefers to spend a care-free life in an unrestrained manner. In other words, he undertakes some special efforts occasionally to accomplish some goal or fulfil his wishes. Therefore one should know what *sadhana* is.

Some people are afraid that they may have to move to jungle or enter into fire and perform many difficult rituals for undertaking sadhana. But man does not understand that daily he performs some sadhana or other during the course of his daily routine works. In other words, we are performing *sadhana* daily but unknowingly. To realise God, no difficult practice is to be specially undertaken. A farmer does so much of sadhana to accomplish his farming work. Even a thief or a pick-pocket learns so many tricks for stealing. Compared to all these, spiritual practice to realise God is easier. God has gifted us with so many divine qualities. Only if we know their importance and try to inculcate those divine qualities in us, we can achieve wonders. Peace and happiness will be within our easy reach.

By doing karma in a proper manner, not only we should survive, but also we should live harmoniously in the society with peace and happiness, and ultimately realise our True Self by acquiring self-knowledge. This should be everyone's karttavya of highest order. Any other type of karma bereft of the above objective will surely bring us bondage and sufferings. Man being the best and most developed creature in this Creation, all his actions should be performed with knowledge and skill. It should be remembered that without sadhana, one cannot possess adequate strength, courage and confidence to accomplish his goal. *Sadhana* enables a man to lead a successful and worthy life.

Skill employed to consciously accomplish a goal smoothly and selflessly in shortest time with minimum cost and labour is known as *sadhana*. Spiritual practice or sadhana is enhanced by renunciation and self-restraint. Renunciation, self-restraint and spiritual practice constitute Karma Yoga. By spiritual practice, self-restraint also gets strengthened. Therefore, self-restraint and spiritual practice are complementary to each other. According to Divya Darshan, whatever karma a man performs in his day to day life, constitutes *sadhana* or spiritual practice although he is not aware of the unknown and distant goal. There is no need to perform any fearsome practice to attain one's True Self. Only if all our karma is streamlined towards a particular goal, success is bound to come on the way. On the other hand, if karma is performed in a whimsical or haphazard manner, there are more chances of failure than of success. We all perform some karma or other. Whatever we do is all karma. But the most pertinent point is- 'What should we do?' The answer is- The goal of attaining true knowledge and

 Sanatan Dharma

realising True Self is the highest karma, Dharma, *Karttavya* and *Sadhana* for a human being who has already been bestowed with inquisitiveness, knowledge and conscience. Hence man should unswervingly tread on the spiritual path and undertake spiritual practices to know his real spiritual identity. This is called true divine life. Karma becomes *sadhana* when karma, linked to the goal, is skilfully performed in a selfless manner without eyeing on the fruits of action. It is called Karma Yoga. The essence of *sadhana* is skill in action linked to the goal. Animals and birds etc. perform their activities with their latent skill. Birds build their nests so skilfully. The white ants build the ant-hills so beautifully. Similarly, the honeybees build their hives with so much of diligence and skill. It is their *sadhana*. Man is endowed with the discriminating faculty to know what good is and what bad is. Only a human being can enquire about his goal. He is endowed with conscience. He gets inspiration and encouragement from within. Good works enhance divine virtues in him. That is why it is said that karma is the cause of bondage; karma is also the cause of freedom. Man becomes more powerful by dint of spiritual practice through karma, bhakti and jnana. Spiritual practice culminates as divine virtues which ultimately lead to attainment of Moksa. Spiritual practice is a path of self-development and the goal is attainment of True Self. By knowledge and spiritual practice, the impossible can be made possible. If anything is considered impossible, it is to be inferred that there is inadequacy of either or both.

SERVICE (SEVA)

Service is God gifted quality which is always functional in this Creation. Nothing is an isolated entity. Everything works in tandem with something or other. Everything is integrated and interwoven with the other. One serves the other. One depends upon another. The plant kingdom draws its sustenance from the mineral kingdom. The animal kingdom cannot survive without the plant kingdom. Multifarious natural ingredients constitute the mineral kingdom. They are at the service of the natural flora and fauna which in turn are engaged in the service of the world. The herbal shrubs are a great boon to us. Even earth, water, light, air etc. always render their services. Without the Sun and Sunlight, the Earth would not have come to existence. We would not have been there; the plant kingdom and the animal kingdom would not have been there. Be it day and night or seasonal changes, everything we get due to regular and timely rotation of the Earth round the Sun.

Service or Seva is so important for our survival. Even to maintain our bodies, we all take care of them regularly. To live harmoniously in the society with peace and happiness to complete the life's journey, we require so many services from others at each stage. Otherwise, our living would have been impossible. We are also expected to serve others when needed. Particularly in old age or while in the hospital for treatment, the indispensability of service is well-experienced. Man is born to move on the path of self-development for which he must possess divine qualities. There are many who, in order to earn virtues, dig wells and ponds for the benefit of others. Some build rest houses, schools, orphanages and hospitals for the service of the people. Thus, people render services to others in several ways. The goal of human life is realisation of True Self. This is liberation. For attainment of this highest goal, all must consciously strive in whatever religions or professions they may be. Therefore, reading scriptures and spreading spiritual knowledge for the self-development of others in the society is also a noble and important service. We should not only walk on the path of Dharma but we should also motivate others to walk on the path of Dharma which is so important for the attainment of life's goal. It is said that service to mankind is service to God.

In our own bodies various limbs work in a mutually supportive manner to serve a common interest. Various systems, which are for blood circulation, food digestion and respiration etc., function so perfectly and incessantly. Most sophisticated parts like brain, heart, liver, lungs and kidney etc. work flawlessly in all of us for which we survive and are kept fit. The parents, however big they may be, serve their children. Even the ferocious tigress feeds her cubs and protects them. Nature provides the life-saving milk in the mother's breast before a baby is born. Sun gives us light, heat, life and energy. Moon sprinkles the subtle and soothing beam and lights the whole earth. The plants consume the carbon di-oxide and release the oxygen for our use. From all these examples, it is quite evident that service is the underlying essential principle in this Creation. Through service, one will be able to get oneself acquainted with higher and higher truths. People serve the nation whether one is a farmer, defence personnel, scientist, teacher, researcher or an artisan. While an educationist educates others by his knowledge, a soldier keeps the whole country secure. Through service, one will be able to get acquainted with higher and higher truths that bring him more knowledge and experience. For example, a scientist carries on various experiments in his laboratory and does so much research, even sacrificing his food and sleep at times. Even if he may not be successful in all his endeavours, his knowledge gets enhanced at every step. That is how he moves on from matters to atoms, and from atoms to protons and from protons to god-particles, thereby unravelling truths one after another. Service is the culmination of Karma Yoga. Therefore, in service, there are both karma and *bhava*. Sattvic qualities develop in the man who serves. Bhakti Yoga begins from seva. Without seva, the life of the living beings would have been miserable. Nature is so bountiful that she feeds one and all and provides all minerals and vitamins for our sustenance. Nature is God's manifestation. God assumes different forms and names, and appears before us as nature, serves us every day by providing refreshing morning, sunshine, colourful flowers, varieties of flavoursome fruits, vegetables, and food grains with so much care and love.

A mother renders desireless service to her children. Services rendered with some motive or with expectation for some return become less effective as they cannot give pure happiness to the recipients. The desire to serve others should come from the core of heart. This is pure and sattvic. The spiritual seekers can very quickly take to desireless service while most of the people render services with desires. One day or other, they will also come to the level of desireless service. As explained in the Shrimad Bhagavad-Gita, Karma Yoga means giving up sense of doership, surrendering all karma to God and finally giving up desire for any fruit. This is called desireless action (karma).

Divya Darshan says, karma in order to be qualitatively better and more productive, must be backed by knowledge and skill. Karma becomes service or seva when it is intended for the well-being of others and self, with the ultimate aim of attaining one's goal of self-realisation. The term, 'others', includes plants, animals and humans. Seva-oriented karma is the karttavya or duty of everybody. In other words, such desireless karma becomes seva, karttavya, sadhana (spiritual practice) and Dharma. That means, if karma is undertaken by someone with knowledge and skill for the wellness of self as well as others i.e. with the attitude of rendering services (seva) to others, it will develop other divine virtues such as truth, love and forgiveness in him, and shall bring him peace, bliss and self-realisation which is the goal of everybody.

By seva, one can get blessings from everyone, i.e. from animal, bird, man and the divine beings. Through and by seva, a man's past sins as well as his bondages can be destroyed in this birth. The importance of seva has been well explained in various scriptures. Seva is the duty (karttavya) and Dharma of everybody. Seva brings self-development. Seva brings peace and bliss. Lord Jesus said, "Love thy neighbour as Thyself." According to Divya Darshan, service and love are complementary to each other. In love, there are seva (service) and bliss. Seva is an effective medium to establish relationship with God. Seva cleans all inner dirt and purifies the man who serves desirelessly. Service does not mean only serving others. Service also means service to the self and God. First, we have to take care of our bodies by cleaning them regularly, take appropriate food and water for their maintenance. We do Yoga and Pranayam. We also do meditation for the stability of mind and intellect. While these are essential, service to God is the best service. Service elevates one to other divine qualities like truth, love and forgiveness which constitute Jnana Yoga according to Divya Darshan. In special circumstances even God incarnates to directly serve mankind by imparting true knowledge by which they can tread on the path of Dharma, get rid of all sufferings, and attain peace, bliss and liberation. The divine quality of seva is there in everybody. It is a God-gifted quality which man possesses since his birth.

TRUTH

It is very difficult to define truth. It is not that easy to decide what is true and what is untrue. The greatness of the term truth is unknown to many. Most of the people know about truth, but in a limited sense. The equivalent of Truth in Sanskrit is 'Satya' which means- "That which was there in the past, is present now and shall exist in future." In other words, Truth is that which always exists. Truth is only eternal. In this world, only truth exists for ever. All others are ephemeral. The world is there due to manifestation of Truth. Whatever is experienced, heard or seen, everything is manifestation of Truth. Therefore, Truth is eternal.

Truth manifests as forms and qualities. On the other hand, Truth which is present as the basis or cause of the names and forms is called Supreme Truth. Our world experience is mainly due to our five sense organs such as eye, ear, nose, tongue and skin. There are some invisible things which the sense organs cannot reach. By knowledge alone, we experience those subtle and invisible things.

Examples: Ice is a truth. Without water, ice would not have been possible. Likewise, water is composed of some gas molecules. This means that water has come from Hydrogen and Oxygen. Without this combination, water or ice would not have been possible. In other words, although ice, water, vapour are truths, they have come from some other truths such as Hydrogen and Oxygen. It is pertinent to note that the Supreme Truth who is there as the Supra-Causal factor cannot be explained by citing any example. Examples can be advanced for the manifested states only. But no example is possible in respect of the Unmanifest who is Unity, Eternity, Infinity and the Indivisible Whole. There is none second to Him.

The Supreme Truth manifests as innumerable truths like forms and qualities. To explain the Supreme Truth and His manifested states, different names such as Brahman, Ishwar, jiva, plants, air, water, earth etc. are ascribed. Truth is present somewhere as the cause, somewhere as karma and somewhere as the result thereof. In this way, the processes of creation, preservation and destruction happen incessantly. This manifestation is generally called as lila. In other words, Truth manifests through lila. The maker of lila is the Supreme Truth. He is the Supra-Causal force and there is none other than Him. Whatever we come across or experience, whether the same is considered by us as good or bad, everything is but truth. There are some favourable situations for the jiva depending on which he survives. When man faces unfavourable situations, according to him, he suffers. This is due to ignorance. He misconstrues something for other due to ignorance as a result of which he gets himself entangled in different situations. It is necessary therefore to know what truth is. Knowing the truth is called true knowledge or right knowledge. By acquiring true knowledge, one can get rid of all sufferings. This Creation is nothing but a manifestation of truth. The Creation is full of truth from the beginning to the end. Everything is regulated by truth. Man is born by truth and survives by truth. He gets happiness, peace and bliss due to truth. Man cannot live even for a moment without truth. Truth exists eternally. Truth is neither created nor destroyed. Realisation of Truth is the greatest bliss. Truth can be explained by truth only.

Different minerals have different properties. Different plants have different characteristics. Different animals have different forms and qualities. Those are all relative truths. The Supreme Truth is the Absolute Truth. He is Brahman who pervades everywhere. He sustains all and protects all. Truth is the life and vital energy of everybody. Truth appears as brother, father, friends and relatives to support us. Truth brings happiness, peace and bliss to everyone. There is truth behind our birth. There is also truth for our death. There is truth for our bondage; there is truth for our freedom. There is truth for our suffering; there is also truth for our peace and bliss. Realisation of truth brings bliss. Without truth, the Creation would not have been possible. Behind all changes, there is Truth which is unchangeable. Truth can be realised by knowledge in *bhava* state, but not by arguments. It is not that easy to realise Truth. By the good impulses acquired during past several births only, there arises inquisitiveness to know what Truth is. Then only one gets some indication of Truth. Truth manifests spontaneously. Not knowing the Truth is ignorance.

It is therefore our first and foremost duty to uphold truth, practise and apply truth. Truth can be realised by truth. Everything becomes possible by truth. Respecting and loving truth is the highest divine quality which one should have. Ultimately you will realise that you are the Truth-Absolute. Never ignore or disrespect truth. If one disrespects truth, the outcome is suffering.

LOVE

This Creation is nothing but God's play or lila. The quality of love has made this Creation livelier and more beautiful. Some people love money; some people love matters, and some people love beautiful creatures. The play of love goes on incessantly in this world, somewhere less and somewhere more depending on the nature and behaviour of the lover and the loved. The quality of love is instinctively present everywhere and in every being. To inculcate the quality of love, no external training is necessary. Everyone has an instinct to get happiness and bliss. That is why there is love which is a divine quality. Where there is love, there is bliss (Ananda). God has gifted love to all of us so that we will be happy and blissful. But due to ignorance, man is not able to understand the value of true love. Had he known what true love is, he would have intensely loved the Creator, the Love-Absolute to enjoy infinite bliss. "God is mine. I am His. His 'Self' and my 'Self' are one and the same. I am That." This blissful state is liberation where there is no fear or anxiety.

Opposite of bliss is suffering. In other words, absence of peace and happiness is called suffering or misery. Due to ignorance of the jiva about his blissful True Self, he suffers. In order to get rid of sufferings, he makes some efforts. Thus, everyone is on his journey towards liberation.

Now the question is- why man is not able to attain that blissful state called liberation? It is because he makes some sporadic attempts lacking sincerity and focus. It must be remembered that love is an essential prerequisite for attaining the blissful state which is liberation. It is regrettable that due to ignorance, man does not understand the value of love. In his day to day life, he entertains the feelings of ego, selfishness, jealousy, anger and greed which are opposite to the quality of love. With such qualities, how can he get peace and happiness? Only by possessing the divine quality of love, one can attain peace and liberation. We are under the wrong impression that man can live happily if he has good amount of material possessions. Had it been so, the kings and emperors would have been the happiest men in this Creation. Only because of their outward splendour they appear to be happy. Even a person with no material wealth can be happy if he possesses the divine quality of love. Let us take the example of the sages who live so happily. They do not have any possession, not even a small hut. Still they live in bliss. A mother loves her child so much. All other material things are insignificant compared to mother's love. Where there is love, there is peace and bliss. So many other qualities like sacrifice, truth, restraint, forgiveness and service remain ingrained in the divine quality of love. In other words, all the divine qualities culminate as love. In absence of love, one has to undergo sufferings throughout. In other words, where there is suffering, there is no love. Due to ignorance, infatuation is misconstrued for love. The tamasic people, who are mostly guided by their mind, rarely differentiate between right and wrong. That is why they suffer. Mind being volatile makes the man restless and unstable. Accordingly, his thoughts also change amazingly fast. Man gets attracted towards a beautiful appearance that makes him happy for some time but when gradually the beauty fades away, he again becomes unhappy. Therefore, a beautiful appearance is not a source of permanent joy.

True love does not know any suffering. True love starts from love for someone's qualities. As explained earlier, love for a beautiful appearance cannot be termed as love. The same is only infatuation. Qualities are subtle and hence last longer. In other words, quality is more beautiful than mere appearance. We might have come across many great personalities who were so much adorable for their knowledge or proficiency. Those, who love qualities more than appearance, are of rajasic nature since they are guided by their intelligence. But this love is not pure love because there remains a hidden element of some expectation. Love that comes from the level of conscience is of sattvic nature. Hence it is superior to the previous ones. We must remember that Atman is more lovable than qualities. Atman is eternal. Hence the love for Atman is eternal and blissful. Further, Atman undergoes no birth, decay or death. There is not an iota of suffering too. Those who love Atman are great. They simultaneously possess the qualities of truth, service, piety and righteousness etc. Due to these divine qualities one becomes eligible to attain Atman. Where there is love but other divine qualities are absent, it means, it is not true love. Such so-called love is either pretentious or deceptive. One cannot get lasting peace or bliss from out of such spurious love. To spread the message of love, great personalities like Lord Jesus and Sri Chaitanya descended on earth to teach mankind what love is. Love is nectar-like. He, who possesses this divine quality, lives in eternal bliss and becomes immortal.

There is nothing to get disheartened. Anybody can attain this stage of love. It is an eternal truth. The basis of bliss is love which is present in everybody. Hence there is no question of not getting the same. The Creation exists due to love. Hence it is not impossible to develop the quality of love from inside. The tigress is so ferocious. But how carefully and lovingly does it bring up its cubs! Had there been no divine quality of love in the mother

 SANATAN DHARMA

tigress, the kids would not have survived. If we look at a bird, we see how sincere and careful it is while building its nest. How it broods over its eggs constantly! How it feeds and protects its offspring! Is it not due to love? How much a mother loves her children! It is a befitting example of desireless and unalloyed love. Even a thief who indulges in wrongdoings loves his kids so much. If any love is driven by selfish desires, it is not pure love.

Desireless love brings peace and bliss. Love gradually rises from the level of intelligence and reaches the level of Atman. This is the culmination of love. Bliss is the outcome. It is Supreme Bliss or Eternal Bliss. So many sages had attained this state after prolonged spiritual practices. The quality of love gets blossomed in one's heart due to God's grace. We love various matters, men and animals but we are not able to love God due to our ignorance. He, who loves God gets rid of all sufferings and becomes Bliss-Absolute.

We must recollect our mother's love and her sacrifice for us. We have survived due to mother's love. All creatures in this Creation have survived due to their mothers' love. This means, there is mother's love behind every life. Love is God gifted. It is the basis of the Creation. Everyone possesses this God-gifted quality from his very birth. By this quality of love, man can realise God ultimately. Once one attains this state, one will be loved by one and all. For him, nothing is impossible. An enemy will become friendly with him. All sufferings shall vanish. He will be the happiest man even if he leads life as a poor householder.

As knowledge increases, sattvic qualities also increase. By sattvic quality, love can be understood. Gradually, this love shall be transformed into universal love. At that time, the jiva will feel as if he is in the ocean of bliss. When the jiva will love Brahman, it is the highest love different from all other types of love. In this state, there does not remain any ill feeling towards anybody or anything. Everything becomes divine.

True nature of love: Jiva is born in bliss. That is why he craves for bliss. By means of love, he enjoys bliss. Therefore, his instinct is to love. There is selfishness in mundane love. Therefore, it is the cause of bondage. When it is extended to universal love or divine love, it brings liberation. There is no selfishness in true love. In true love, there remains no expectation, no grudge, or any type of non-fulfilment. There is no desire for any wealth or fame, not even liberation. His happiness is my happiness; His wills and instructions are only to be fulfilled or carried out by me. What else is there to offer to Him other than Self? In other words, complete and unconditional self-surrender is true love. He, who loves the Truth-Absolute, becomes blissful. It is nothing but loving the Self. This highest love culminates in union with Brahman. There remains only unity without any diversity. I am the Love-Absolute, Bliss-Absolute and Truth-Absolute Self: manifested as the Creation. This is realisation of True Self, or liberation. The Self, through lila, loves the Self and gets united with the Self who is blissful and eternal.

The role and importance of Love: He, who possesses the divine quality of love, gets rid of all sufferings and realises True Self. All accumulated *vikaras* are destroyed at the magic touch of true love. In love, the importance of renunciation is quite evident. All disharmony and discord vanish where love rules. Love can achieve wonders that any material wealth cannot achieve. Love is the Grace of God. Hence love is so powerful. Bliss is the outcome of love. Nothing remains unattained where there is love. The Creation is sustained by love. Without it, everything would have been disintegrated and destroyed. Love is the most powerful tool for God-realisation. There is no other divine quality stronger than love.

Love from spiritual angle: Brahman is Ahladini Shakti. This Shakti is the power to attract one and all towards itself (Brahman). This force contains love and love contains attractive force. Love and attraction are one and the same. This is present everywhere and in everything. True nature of love is inexplicable or inexpressible. It can only be experienced. It is called infinite love, celestial love or divine love. Atman is unitary but manifests in different stages and appears many. There is gold but when it appears in different designs as ornaments, it looks more attractive. Love is like that. It appears differently in different beings like love between husband and wife, brother and sister, mother and child etc. Love also expresses itself through different forms and qualities. The sages had realised this and that is why they loved God as well as all beings. They loved the whole universe as divine manifestation.

The term 'love', due to ignorance, is not understood properly. The mundane love ends up with sufferings whereas the divine love is always blissful. Man attains this highest state of love only by divine grace. God is Love-Absolute and Bliss-Absolute. Without His grace, man cannot love Him. He, who loves Him, attains Him. At that time, there is no end to the love and there is no end to the bliss. Man gets lost in bliss. Everything becomes still and silent. Only blissful tears roll out from the realiser.

FORGIVENESS

It is the best and highest among all divine qualities. All *vikaras* vanish when the spiritual mendicant attains the state of forgiveness. As a result of all spiritual practices, the mendicant attains this state and realises his goal of self-realisation. Forgiveness is a divine quality that is spontaneous. This quality is not learnt and acquired. It is a gift of nature and therefore it spontaneously appears in the spiritual seeker. Had there been no divine quality like forgiveness, the earth would have been destroyed long ago.

A tiger is ferocious. But it tolerates all nuisances made by its cubs. It does not kill them. A mother smilingly tolerates and forgives her child who is so naughty and troublesome. It is a God-gifted instinct in the mother to forgive her children. Other accompanying qualities of forgiveness are service, truth and love. Forgiveness comes because of love. The seeker thereafter reaches nirvikar state and gets rid of all worldly sufferings.

Forgiveness is the highest strength and a supreme quality. This divine quality puts out all negative qualities such as greed, jealousy and intolerance. It is so powerful that it can captivate the whole world even. Forgiveness is a powerful asset that leads to God-realisation. Forgiveness is synonymous with happiness, peace and bliss. It qualifies the seeker to reach the highest goal which he has been craving for so long.

Instead of forgiveness, when man becomes a prey to the demoniac qualities like revengefulness, he burns himself in the fire of anger, jealousy and crookedness, and thereby he suffers a lot. His counterpart will also be reactive and revengeful and inflict pain on him. In such situation, where is peace? One must be free from all *vikaras*. By this, the way to liberation will be clear. One will have equal vision towards everybody. There is God in all beings and everywhere. This feeling will come to him consequently. To reach this state, a spiritual speaker has to make lot of spiritual practice with great amount of sincerity and love. The sages could reach such a state with lot of perseverance. Lord Jesus had forgiven the miscreants even when he was being crucified. The great Socrates forgave the persons who made him drink the poison hemlock. Swami Dayananda, the founder of Arya Samaj and a great reformer had asked the person, who poisoned him to death, to immediately leave the place lest he should be caught and punished by his disciples. Men of such heights behaved in such manner very naturally and spontaneously and not for the sake of forgiveness. A mother forgives her child. It may not be that much unalloyed. She is conscious that the child is born of her. Therefore, natural love comes from the mother to the child. This also becomes a cause of bondage for her. But the feelings of the sages are different which cannot be expressed in any language. The sages have transcended all bondages and reached this highest state. They are liberated souls. Although they appear to dwell in samsar, they do not get afflicted by samsaric Maya. They are one with the Truth-Absolute.

Now the question may arise as to whether a common man can rise to this state. The answer is 'Yes'. When the Creator has gifted these qualities to man, why can't it be possessed? One can very well observe this quality in a mother. A spiritual seeker has to learn this quality from a mother first and thereafter gradually he can reach nirvikar state. A seeker thereafter can attain liberation and get rid of all worldly sufferings. Forgiveness is Peace-Absolute, Bliss-Absolute and Truth-Absolute. This is such a divine quality that it ensures man's survival, peace, happiness and bliss. Ultimately, the jiva experiences that "I am Sat-Chit-Ananda".

It all starts from renunciation which is there in the first segment of the monogram. Man can blossom himself by this divine quality of renunciation and attain perfection in forgiveness, the ultimate divine quality free from all *vikaras*.

Just like seven colours i.e. VIBGYOR, the seven divine qualities are also intertwined and are complementary to each other.

To elucidate further, without the quality of renunciation, self-restraint is not possible. In other words, renunciation is the basis of self-restraint. Similarly, spiritual practice gets enhanced by the quality of self-restraint. Spiritual practice makes the seeker strong enough to do service to others. He will gradually understand that by 'Truth' everything happens. There is truth behind everything. Therefore, service is a means to establish direct contact with truth. Man thus realises the Supreme Truth ultimately. That is why it is said that service to mankind is service to God. Going further, Truth is the basis of love. One gets attracted towards another person after experiencing some truths in the other. Love means loving some truths. In other words, truth finds expression as love. Forgiveness is the spontaneous offshoot of love. Love is the basis of forgiveness. Where there is love, there is no malice or deceitfulness. The lover can surrender everything for the sake of the beloved. The lover becomes free from all *vikaras*.

Like this, all divine qualities are there in man. God has gifted all these divine qualities to man so that he can get back to True Self. But due to ignorance, man is not able to realise the importance of the divine qualities. Rather he pursues the demoniac qualities due to which he suffers throughout.

Light contains seven colours. Without light, there will be darkness everywhere. Similarly, without divine qualities, man will be in dark. He goes on cursing darkness instead of welcoming light. With all divine qualities in him, he can shine bright like the Sun.

The greatness of divine qualities: Man gets peace and happiness due to divine qualities. Conversely, he suffers due to demoniac qualities. Man's survival is possible due to divine qualities. Divine qualities are everlasting assets which never get lost or diminished unlike the material wealth. The impossible can be made possible by divine qualities. Man gets all his inspiration and encouragement due to the divine qualities. Besides the aforesaid seven divine qualities, faith, trust, inquisitiveness and humility etc. are also divine qualities. Man proceeds on the path of self-development and ultimately realises True Self due to divine qualities. Divine qualities are nectar-like that bring peace and bliss, life and lustre. Possessing divine qualities is the highest Dharma. Truth prevails where there are divine qualities. Without divine qualities, the family and society will stand disintegrated. Divine qualities are the light of life. Blessings, greetings, gratitude and goodwill etc. are the outcome of divine qualities. Divine qualities lead us to heaven whereas demoniac qualities lead to hell. Man has the option to choose between divine qualities and demoniac qualities. All spiritual seekers, after their intense spiritual practice, gain divine qualities as a result of which they attain the supreme goal of life. Divine qualities are very much active in the kingdom of nature. The Law of Eternity works only on the basis of divine qualities. In other words, the Creation exists and is sustained by divine qualities.

 SANATAN DHARMA

AMRITBINDU

Man's ultimate aim is to get peace and bliss. This becomes possible only if he enjoys unfettered freedom from bondage. It is ignorance only, which is primarily responsible for reducing man to a mere bundle of desires. Ignorance is synonymous with "not knowing the truth". That is why, man gropes in darkness and craves for all other things except his own 'self'.

'Self' is the only source of light and knowledge. Self is the only knowable essence to be discovered by the self. In absence of self-knowledge, ignorance reigns supreme. As a result sorrows and suffering stem out of ignorance.

Likewise, Sadguru Sri Sri Arjun (1933-1989) gave the mankind His "Divya Darshan" or "The Philosophy Divine" which is an integrated philosophy on Karma, Bhakti and *Jnana*. Divya Darshan, a product of the Law of Eternity also contains within it the Law of Eternity and takes care of the total need of the mankind by its lucid expression.

Sadguru Sri Sri Arjun says, "Knowing the Law of eternity is *Dharma*". Without observance of *Dharma*, peace and bliss will remain a far cry. Man's sufferings unmistakably indicate that there is breach of *Dharma*. Amrit Bindu presents a few nectarine droplets which may help in accelerating man's inward journey towards that Eternal Abode where all paths and all journeys get blissfully merged.

1. Ignorance is the cause of misery.

2. True, you never welcome sufferings. Only your ignorance brings them to you. You are absolutely divine. Therefore, pursue divine knowledge, desire only divinity

and engross yourself in divine thoughts and then only Divine Bliss will be bestowed upon you.

3. Ignorance breeds sin. Sin breeds sorrows. Hence welcome knowledge and get rid of all sufferings.

4. Matter can be understood by tuition and God's greatness by (spiritual) intuition.

5. Dharma emanates from knowledge [jnana] and liberation [moksa] from Dharma.

6. Nurturing 'ego' due to ignorance, the jive considers himself big but the more he realises the greatness of God, the more he gets convinced about his own ineffectiveness and considers himself more and more insignificant. The more insignificant you will consider yourself the more significant you will be adjudged as, because by this, you are becoming worthy of blessings from the Divine Power.

7. Doubts and despair, fear and distress are directly proportional to ignorance, and to get rid of all these, it is inevitable to seek protection from someone else. Therefore dispel your ignorance, tide over all these nightmares and be blessed, realizing the greatness of Jnana Shakti.

8. Ignorance breeds fear. Ignorance prompts a man to tread on forbidden tracks only to pluck bitter fruits. Ignorance enshrouds the true self and causes rebirths. Therefore enrich yourself with true knowledge, get rid of fear and anxieties, know your Self and attain immortality.

9. Who is immune from all fears and anxieties? He, who has surrendered himself to the supreme and got His blessings

10. Great indeed you are! Divine Bliss is your birth right. Man is a superb creation and after innumerable transmigrations he is embodied in this rare and fair from.

11. You are the source of all energy. Therefore pursue yourself, awaken yourself and illumine yourself.

12. Live not a dull and drab life. Containing that divine ocean of love nectar in yourself, profusely pour out the same over the creation. "Behold! The entire creation is flooded with nectar and you will thus be merged one day with the supreme bliss by getting a taste of the love nectar. That is but the real goal of life"

13. This is no life at all. To know the infuser of life is true life.

14. When you realise that God's grace is being showered upon you every moment and you are being regulated by Him, it is to be understood that you have become equal minded. Therefore peace is inevitable.

15. Where is shraddhaa without faith? Where is bliss without contemplating on Brahman? Where is Moksa without self-surrender?

16. If you want to live, be dutiful. If you want peace and happiness, possess divine virtues. If you desire liberation, acquire self-knowledge.

17. Everyone craves for mastering fortune but fails. Because none can acquire fortune by dint of vices. It becomes possible only by divine qualities. Oh mankind! Possessing divine qualities is Dharma. Dharma is the key to all fortunes.

18. To repose faith on God (Truth) is the first and foremost Dharma. To do good or wish good to others, sacrificing self-interest is the second Dharma. To live (righteously) while letting others live is the third Dharma. Unmindful of whether others live or not but only mindful of "Live I must" cannot find a place in any category of Dharma.

19. Your true self is not this. Your true self is Sat-Chit-Anand (Existence, knowledge and bliss). In the darkness of ignorance, you are unable to know your true self. Therefore enkindle the light of knowledge within, know yourself and free yourself from all miseries.

20. He is greater than what we know Him as. It is impossible to realise Him without His grace.

21. To reach God or to get Him, no qualification is necessary but to win His Grace it is essential to have some qualification. Hence be worthy of God's Grace.

22. Arise and awake! Gird up your loins to reach the goal. 'Karma' is Sadhana, 'Karma' is life and 'Karma' is bliss (Ananda).

23. How the fruits of actions are enjoyed can be understood once one realises one's own self.

24. Too much of obsession with the matter makes you insentient. It is to be accepted that only spiritual knowledge frees oneself from the clutches of matter.

25. It is not that easy to know Truth. A glimpse of the Supreme Truth can be had only when inquisitiveness springs up due to the good impulses (samskara) acquired through many births.

26. Truth is self-illumined. None else illumines Him. But the ignorant man cannot know Truth. To know Him pursue knowledge, pursue truth and practise truth.

27. Uphold Truth; apply Truth since Truth can be had by Truth alone. Whatever is possible is achieved by Truth only.

28. Truth is nectar; falsehood poison.

29. Falsehood proves nothing; Truth proves everything.

30. Have faith in Truth. Love Truth and respect Truth. Truth is the governing principle of your life. All excellence of your life is contained in it. It is your true self.

31. We are bred by Truth, brought up by Truth and shall be sustained by Truth. Defying Truth means advancing towards hell which is nothing but suicide.

32. Divine you are. Divinity is your goal. Divinity is your base. Divine is your life and divine is your true self.

33. Self-knowledge never comes by mere listening or reading. It dawns upon one who gets engrossed in repeated contemplation on the Supreme.

34. Atman cannot be known by mind or intelligence. Conscience gets some indication of it. It is only by Atman that Atman can be known. "Not mind, not intelligence, not conscience but I am only Atman."

When this thought dawns upon, Atman can be known by Atman.

35. Jnana is a mirror by which you see yourself and others.

36. By Jnana and Sadhana, the impossible can be made possible. If anything appears impossible, it is to be inferred that there is inadequacy of either or both.

37. Truth exists in everything. Real peace comes on realising Truth.

38. The equilibrating state of mind, intelligence and conscience is peace. Conflicts occur when they are in disequilibrium.

39. Mind cannot be restrained unless strong faith is reposed on the supreme.

40. The more the mind is stilled, the greater is the happiness. More stability of knowledge and mind brings more and more bliss.

41. Truth is peace. Truth is bliss and Truth is the basis of moksa.

42. Truth is something, which is not reached easily. If chased, it moves farther. Remember, He is very near to you. He is the heart of your heart and life of your life. Everything in you is manifested by Him. You are not able to understand Him due to ignorance. Once you welcome Him, He will spontaneously come to you in different forms. At last you will realise that "He is I and I am He." In other words, "I am the Brahman i.e. Aham Brahmosmi."

43. He is Truth; He is Knowledge; He is Bliss Absolute. The basis of all that we see in this creation is He, the Supreme Being. Therefore, surrender unto Him and attain the highest.

44. From knowledge of the Supreme comes faith; from faith comes devotion; from devotion come blessings. Hence it matters little whether you ascribe any form to the Supreme or believe in His formlessness. You should gather knowledge of the Supreme in order to gain faith and devotion by which you will get His blessings.

45. Jnana culminates in love and love in bliss. Hence, acquire true knowledge and enjoy Supreme Bliss.

46. By jnana, the standpoints of others and self can be known. Therefore why negligent in enkindling the latent knowledge in you to know your true self? Remember! You are the Knowledge-Absolute.

47. We always speak of 'I' but who is that 'I', we never try to know. What else can be more shameful and tragic than this? It should be remembered that the knower of the self is the knower of all.

48. We try to know others but never ourselves. This is the main cause of bondage.

49. If you crave for release (Mukti), pursue knowledge of the Supreme. Jnana brings sense of discrimination and makes one clean and pure. Ignorance makes one impure. Therefore purify yourself by acquiring Jnana and realise your true Self.

50. We are keen to clean our bodies but we never make our mind clean. To an impure, everything appears impure. Therefore mind has to be cleansed along with the body.

51. First, purify your heart. God will be reflected on a pure heart. Instead of worshipping Him in our heart, if we worship Him outwardly by arranging for Him decorative seats, flowers and sandal wood etc., then what to speak of fulfilling our desires, it will amount to self-deceit and misleading others too.

52. Try to understand Him whom you worship. Without knowing Him if you expect anything from Him, remember, all your worship has gone in vain.

53. By mere outward worship, you do not get His blessings. Only by strong faith and sincere obedience to His Will, His blessings shall be showered upon you.

54. Only he who cannot beg anything of Him reaches Him. He, who begs, gets only the desired objects, instead of getting Him.

55. Knowing Him, and His greatness and thereafter conducting oneself in tune with His Will pay much more than merely worshipping and asking for something.

56. God is realised by Jnana. This so called Jagat is nothing but His True Self.

57. It is not necessary to search for God outside. All our visions and thoughts are His manifestations. In other words, He Himself is all thoughts and expressions. Therefore, He is not something to be searched out but only to be realised.

58. Know the truth to know the Supreme.

59. Knowing is becoming. The knower of Atman therefore gets immerged with the all-pervasive Atman.

60. The Supreme is beyond contemplation. Contemplation is His mere play (Lila). Remember! The universe, which appears real to us, is only a product of Lila. But He Himself is more real than the visible and the invisible universe.

61. His true Self cannot be realised unless we know both the gross and the subtle. Therefore, know both the gross and the subtle to know the Absolute and liberate yourself

62. He alone, who knows Him as both expressible and inexpressible, knows the Absolute.

63. It is better to realise Him by Jnana than to visualise only His gross form, because gross form is only a modified state of His Lila or Maya.

64. There is Maya in Lila. Behind the Lila is its maker. Unless He is understood, Maya cannot be comprehended.

65. There pervades Jnana in Lila. The maker of Lila cannot be known by Jnana. To know the maker of Lila, it is essential to reach the transcendental state which is beyond Jnana. On reaching there, when He and His Lila is realised, then only the jiva frees himself of Maya.

66. Varieties in Lila create the ideas of dualities but on knowing the maker of Lila, all dualities disappear, yielding place to monism (Adwait). Then only the Jiva gets mingled with the One. Hence, Oh seeker of truth! Try to know the maker of Lila instead of getting lost in Lila.

67. Brahman is one not two. The One only appears as many. Those who take Brahman as many, realise neither Brahman nor His Lila.

68. Brahman is beginningless and endless too, neither created nor destroyed.

69. Everything has a comparison but the Absolute Truth has none. Therefore to get Him, He has to be realised by detachment from worldly thoughts. Then only He Himself will unveil and appear before you.

70. Whatever man desires, he gets. Whatever he gets comes to light. Therefore be glad of getting that Eternity, Truth and Bliss and make others attain such excellence.

71. Be happy, be delighted because God has designed the creation to suit all your needs and bestowed upon you the required knowledge.

72. Your creator is also your liberator.

73. Oh mankind! Are miseries, misfortunes and fear of death your ultimate goal? Do these represent your true self? Never, all these are only the outcome of your ignorance. When you can realise your true self by Jnana you will feel that you are pure and pious, wise and immortal.

74. Sensual pleasures are momentary, always dogged by miseries. Renunciation gives real happiness i.e. the Supreme Bliss.

75. What is renunciation? He who has realised, "I am different from this body", has truly renounced to some extent.

76. If you brought nothing while you came, how do you cherish the desire to carry things when you quit? Things you have collected here are to be left here, but you have omitted to collect those things, which you can carry along with you. Those are good knowledge, good deeds, good thoughts and good contemplation.

77. Everybody wants to be happy, free from miseries, misfortunes and maladies holding fast a sense of belongingness. Once the feeling that another power injects life into this life dawns on, the man can be immune from all such sufferings and be immortal.

78. The life as you understand is not true life because that life is followed by death. The realization that you are immortal, pure, pious and blissful is true life.

79. You are a part and parcel of that inexhaustible power. You are wandering aimlessly and leading a wretched life being estranged from Him. Oh mankind! Trace Him out after knowing the Matri Shakti. Then only you will derive power from Him and ultimately free yourself from all miseries.

80. Who is powerful? (a) The Jnani (b) Who upholds love (c) Who serves with dedication (d) Who forgives with an equal vision (e) Who crowns himself with feeling of devotion (f) Who embraces truth and applies the same (g) The vanquisher of the passions

81. By whatever name you may call Him, you are being blessed and controlled by God. While denying this, remember, if you are denuded of all wealth, you will

have nothing to claim as your own. Hence, have faith, have devotion to God.

82. If man cannot believe even after witnessing the play of the Supreme in guise of this universe, then what else he need to see to believe? Not being able to believe can be attributed to ignorance. Just as a child cannot understand himself and the world, likewise man cannot believe God since he does not understand Him due to his ignorance.

83. The knower of Dharma does get the Truth.

84. He is truly Dharmic who observes the spirit of Dharma and not he who merely unfurls the banner of Dharma.

85. Dharma protects us if we protect Dharma.

86. Liberation is inevitable for the observer of Dharma. But indulging ourselves in activities opposite to Dharma, we weep and afterwards crave for God's shelter to save ourselves. Will it really help us? To save ourselves, we must confess our mistakes, swear not to repeat it and follow the path of Dharma. Remember, "As you sow, so you reap".

87. Release from miseries comes from the knowledge of the Supreme. Therefore, Oh mankind! Acquire self-knowledge and free yourselves from miseries.

88. Whatever you say that you know is reflected in your conduct, if it is not, it is to be inferred that you have assimilated very little.

89. The more one gathers knowledge about Dharma, the more one can know and understand truth, which will ultimately lead one to realisation.

90. Peace and bliss go together with Dharma, because Dharma protects us, sustains us and liberates us. Wherever any deviation is marked, it is to be concluded that there is breach of Dharma in its observance either by self or by others. Therefore, carefully understanding its importance, corrective steps should be initiated.

91. When the Jnani himself often fails to understand Dharma, what to speak of the intellectual (vidwan). The basic fact is that unless elevated to super-conscious state, Dharma cannot be realised in its totality.

92. Truth can be known by Jnana. Vidya gives an indication of that Truth.

93. Truth remains at a distant horizon unless the egotism of knowledge is cast off, since whatever we know is negligible. Real Truth is beyond all Jnana.

94. Stop killing the Truth on the pretext of duty because there is Truth in duty. Therefore try to appreciate the Truth.

95. The dutiful alone owns life and is able to get the Truth. Misery and fear remain far away from the dutiful.

96. Waste not your time. That is the source of all magnificence and the yardstick of life. In other words, every moment is invaluable and nectar like.

97. Be not desperate. Success and failure are the two dimensions of Karma. If Karma be your duty, accomplishment of the ultimate goal is inevitable.

98. Man enjoys the fruits of his actions. Hence, well-thought-out deeds must be done.

99. Don't take others as witnesses since you are yourself the doer and also the enjoyer of fruits. You are yourself your witness and in the court of the Supreme, only you are to depose for yourself.

100. "Change" is the best and the strongest proof of God's existence.

101. The Brahman can be realised by a spirit of total self-surrender along with homage of Atman.

102. Know the creator, and you can know the tit-bits of His creation.

103. Humbleness is strength. The more humble a man is, the more powerful he is. Therefore humbleness characterises a powerful man.

104. Be wisely submissive. Be not rigid but be a firm believer. Welcome criticism and make self-introspection.

105. Not to know God is no big lapse but not remembering Him is.

106. By self-realisation, Truth expresses itself as Bliss.

107. The real peace comes from self-knowledge. When the sub-stratum of everything is Atman, how can there be final solution without knowing Him?

108. Truth expresses itself as Existence, knowledge and Bliss. Chi-Shakti is Jnana; Jnana is bliss. Oh mankind! Acquire knowledge and attain the Absolute Bliss.

109. Do good to the society by noble thoughts, noble deeds, and noble advices.

110. Guna excels appearance, jnana excels Guna and God excels jnana. In other words, God manifests Himself as

Rupa, Guna and jnana. Hence the Jnani, on realising God becomes entitled to all excellence.

111. In spite of all virtues, you are unable to know yourself due to the shadow of ignorance, which is like the darkness beneath the lamp. Therefore radiate yourself more and more. Be subtler from subtle. By subtlety alone, you can penetrate into everything and merge yourself with it. Remember, the subtle has no shadow, but the gross has.

112. Until a sense of love has sprouted in your heart, how can you know Him and His love towards you? Therefore, make your heart soft, compassionate and pure by which you can realise His love.

113. Our knowledge is improper and meaningless if we do not have sense of love and devotion towards God. It is only by Jnana that we know God's greatness and as a result, sense of devotion comes in our heart. In the next stage, devotion (Bhakti) is transformed into love (Prema). Once there is love towards God, there is no necessity of Jnana.

114. He is the real devotee who is keen to follow God's instructions.

115. He is great who reposes faith on God and loves Him, because faith paves the way to God and by a sense of love, both Anand and Moksa come forth.

116. Words without love, awareness without Truth become poison. Everything becomes nectarine only by love and truth.

117. There is a name in thought (Bhava) and thought in name. Therefore, reflect upon Name and have the excellence of the nectarine awareness therein.

118. Goal is not achieved without duty. Inquisitiveness and contemplation pave the way clear to the Goal.

119. Contemplate well and in depth and pursue Truth. Be confident that you will get it.

120. Change your mind if you want to be free from sin because when mind changes, everything also changes.

121. Man becomes lovable by casting off ego, free from grief by giving up anger, affluent by relinquishing the desires, happy by giving up greed.

122. Innermost feelings buoy up as your conduct. Conduct reveals one's personality.

123. Love others if you yearn for good will; be truthful and humble if you want blessings; hold unto love if you want bliss; try to know your true self if you want liberation (Mukti).

124. Arguments yield no answers but questions do.

125. Enmity cannot be conquered by enmity but by amity. Therefore true victory lies in conquest of heart and not simply in claiming superiority in a particular situation. Situation changes when heart is conquered.

126. Appearance is no credential. It is Karma alone that speaks for oneself.

127. Confession is not cowardice; it is welcoming the truth.

128. Oh mankind! It is meaningless and wasteful to talk high of others or to indulge in self-adulation. It is Karma

only that reveals one's person and potency. Therefore Karma is the yardstick of life.

129. Where there is wealth, there is bliss. If you are the source of all wealth, Oh Almighty! You are but blissful.

130. Any badness triggered off by you to harm others will ultimately hit you. Therefore abstain from badness forthwith.

131. The ignorant lose temper at once as they are incapable of understanding truth. They cannot appreciate the essence in confessing the wrong as wrong.

132. Arguments beget arguments but not Truth. Truth can be had by a sincere mendicant who gets engrossed in repeated contemplation

133. It is shameful to criticize or praise other religions without following one's own religion. Therefore, be keen to observe own Dharma after knowing what it is.

134. He only tries to find other's mistakes who himself commits mistakes.

135. Stricken by sufferings, man seeks an escape from desires. This paves the way to Godhood, but the affluent in their cravings for luxuries and sensual pleasures plunge into the frying cauldrons of desires as a result of which the way to Godhood gets blocked and they remain away from God.

136. Who is really dearest to God? He, who works to fulfil God's will with all sincerity.

137. One speaks out within the range of one's knowledge. When one strongly feels that some more remain to be learnt, refinement is inevitable.

138. Who is the real hero? He, who is not afraid of death and is firm in fulfilling God's mission braving all odds

139. Man ultimately seeks the protection of truth to get rid of miseries arising out of falsehood. Had he followed truth from the beginning, he would not have been a victim to miseries. This is due to his ignorance.

140. There are many who feel proud of not eating fish or meat, onion or garlic but they have no sincerity for acquiring true knowledge.

141. Always look for the good, as it helps you move higher and higher. But if you see evils, evils will enter into you and cause your downfall.

142. A father has equal vision towards his children. So has God. But man, by the fruits of his actions, enjoys pleasure and pain, until he offers all fruits of actions to God. It is tragic that the ignorant man mistakes himself as the doer of Karma and enjoyer of fruits.

143. If you are unable to understand the latent power of the visible man even after establishing close contact with him, how will you understand the invisible divine power?

144. Where there is dualism there is debate. But monism (Adwait) and debate do not stay together.

145. The Absolute Truth appears when doubts and debates disappear.

146. 'Form' may be a medium for the ignorant to understand things but for somebody who is blind from birth, how can forms help to explain? Therefore jnana is essential both for explaining and understanding.

147. Men of ordinary knowledge are attracted towards appearance, the wise towards qualities but the sages realising Atman in transcendental state get attracted towards Atman.

148. Ego blocks the way to self-realisation but fades away on the advent of true knowledge. Therefore everyone should acquire that True knowledge.

149. Destruction of body is not death. To get upset with misery and fear is death.

150. Knowledge is greater than wealth because wealth is protected by us and we are protected by knowledge.

151. The more the doubts, the more one becomes lifeless. The more one has knowledge, the more one blossoms with life and lustre.

152. He gets something who desires after knowing. He loses who desires without knowing.

153. Who is a Jnani? He, who knows that there is much more than what he knows and affirms that knowing the Absolute is the "True knowledge", is a Jnani indeed. He, who holds an opposite view, is steeped in ignorance.

154. True knowledge never comes until the ego of knowledge is cast off.

155. The best offering is sharing of knowledge. The best virtue is acquisition of knowledge.

156. Capability to understand truth is knowledge.

157. You benefit more by knowing more about Him.

158. Whoever belittles knowledge, belittles God.

159. Whoever receives the blessings of his parents shall receive the blessings of God.

160. Unless one knows the fourth state of matter he cannot understand Para Vidya. God can be realised only with Para Vidya

161. This creation is the manifestation of consciousness. Consciousness is attributeless (nirguna) and dimensionless (nirakara). Gross world is but manifestation of atoms and molecules. Consciousness (chetana) has manifested through a set of rules. These set of rules is known as Sanatan Dharma or Sanatan Niyama

162. Peace cannot be established in the world without divine knowledge and development of divine qualities in the human society

163. To know God is to know the good. Whoever tries to know what is good will realise God. Some mendicants do sadhana to realise God but they do not try to know what is good. As a result they are not able to realise God nor are they happy. It is to be remembered that if man desires to be in a state of bliss, he has to know what is Good which is the root of bliss

164. Knowing the eternal law is knowledge and observing the same is Dharma

165. Whatever we experience through our mind, intellect and senses is known as enjoyment.

166. Never restrict yourself to reading and listening; delve deep into the inner meaning. Never confine yourself to mere speeches but express *jnana* in your conduct. Remember that *Sadhana* brings in humbleness, submissiveness and truthfulness. If these traits are not reflected in your conduct, all your *Sadhana* has been a waste.

167. Unless one is ever watchful, he cannot realise God

Epilogue

When we talk of matter and energy, they are not actually two. They are one and the same but in different states. This means the total energy is monistic. Consciousness is also one and indivisible. Here also there is monistic or non-dual presence of Consciousness. The power of consciousness is the greatest power because we cognize, conceptualize and control all forms of energy by Consciousness only. Therefore consciousness and power are one and the same. It has been also termed by the spiritual scientists as Conscious Energy or Energetic Consciousness. It is all-pervasive. It spontaneously expresses itself in everything whether living or non-living according to circumstances. An example may be cited here. Fire exists everywhere in latent form. When a friction occurs or we strike a match stick, it spontaneously manifests as flame. Likewise, the Almighty is present everywhere unnoticeably but essentially. He manifests as many. He manifests both as visible and invisible.

Energy cannot exist and function intelligently and independently. There must be someone who wields and regulates energy and triggers the process of change by his Will and manifests as many. This means there is homogeneity only behind all apparent heterogeneities

When somebody asks us what is your dharma, the questioner means it to be religion and we also answer in terms of our religion. But religion is not Dharma. Religion is a set of practices which changes over a period of time depending on the requirements of the prevailing customs and times.

But true Dharma is that which remains unchanged forever. We are not taught about true Dharma. We are not taught about the true goal of our life. We are not taught about our true identity. Even we do not know how to conduct ourselves in this world constantly keeping the goal in mind so as to rid ourselves of all sufferings and attain bliss and freedom. These thoughts should agitate us. The journey to self-identity begins with being inquisitive about self.

How does Sadguru help? Once this inner urge to know about self becomes strong, we search for answers. It is said that when the inner inquisitiveness becomes strong, Sadguru finds you. Only one has to recognise Him. He alone can guide us who has completed this journey and has found out the right answer. He enhances our capability to understand things. He clarifies our doubts and delusions (*bhranti*). He is a beacon who guides at various steps in our self-journey. The journey has to be undertaken by self only. There is no substitute for that.

And how does Divya Darshan help? Divya Darshan is the philosophy of life that states the purpose of life and how to conduct oneself in this world. Divya Darshan teaches how to live in the society with harmony, inculcating divine virtues and practising self-knowledge. Divya Darshan asserts with irrefutable logic that we are all divine but since we have taken human forms we have forgotten our True Self. By spiritual efforts and Guru's grace, it is possible to realise our true nature.

Dharma is complex and difficult to explain. It presupposes some basic knowledge. Sadguru Sri Sri Arjun has explained the concept of Dharma in a simple and easy to understand language. This book is a compilation of His teachings. This book is an addition to the already available literatures on this subject. But the style of presentation is simple and hence it is expected that this will be easy to understand Dharma.

As silence cannot be explained by words, likewise, infinity cannot be comprehended by finite. Printed book has its limitations. But he, who follows the teachings and contemplates deeply, may by His grace understand Dharma and realise True Self in this birth itself.

Acknowledgement

Ever since I was inducted into the Sangha, i.e. in the year 1984, on being initiated by Sadguru Sri Sri Arjun, the founder of Divya Darshan Sangha, I have been sincerely learning this unique philosophy and getting inspiration from Sadguru to spread his light of knowledge far and wide for the benefit of people. Divya Darshan believes in unity and not in any sectarianism. It is for the whole of humanity who should know the purpose of human birth, duties and responsibilities, common goal of life, right way of living for pursuing the goal etc.

Nature and God - these two terms are still quite mysterious for most of us and therefore yet to be understood and appreciated by many. A purposeless journey is not only wasteful but dangerous too. Caught in the darkness of ignorance and consequently dipped in sins, we cannot expect peace and happiness. Who can get comfort while sitting over a volcano? It is only by knowledge and divine virtues that we can find peace and bliss within. The Creator's Eternal Law behind His scheme of things must be known first in order to ensure a flawless observance. Trespassers are certainly prosecuted here or here-after under the Law of Karma. Innumerable births are gone, many more are still to come. In this Creation, whatever exists, shall exist without any extinction but with transformations. Play of Energy and Consciousness is wonderful and beyond human understanding for they both are timeless. Nature was there before we were born. Dharma was there before we were born. Brahman willed and manifested as many. The course of the manifestation that includes creation, operation and dissolution, is always governed by the Law of Eternity which is the ageless Sanatan Dharma. Therefore, Dharma upholds us, sustains us, gives us peace and bliss. Dharma ultimately gives us freedom i. e. freedom from all sufferings, freedom from the chain of birth and death and freedom from all bondages. This principle is eternal, universally applicable in all phases and categories of modifications and evolutions until the final destination is attained. Therefore, Dharma is not an individual option but of universal application in the kingdom of nature.

I am ever grateful to my spiritual master who has chosen me as an instrument to embark upon this noble spiritual exercise of spreading true knowledge in the society for the ultimate attainment of peace, bliss and freedom. They will realise who will try to know. It is his, who knows it.

Sisters and brothers of our Sangha pressurised me to bring out one more book focussing on Sanatan Dharma which is the need of the hour considering the chaotic world scenario when life tends to become meaningless and also purposeless. I consider their pressure on me as Gurudev's instruction. I am grateful to one and all.

I must make a special mention about my friend Er. B. P. Mishra ji who extended his fullest cooperation in all matters for an early publication of this book. I am now at 74. My vision is getting blurred. Deceleration process has cast its shadow on me long since. I start, Guru in Mr. Mishra finishes. I sleep, he wakes me up. I am grateful to Er. B. P. Mishra.

My relation with Notion Press, Chennai dates back 2017. I am very much thankful to the Notion Press management and publishing team for their excellent support all along.

All readers are my gods. My salutations to all of you.

Let everyone think good and be good. Let everyone be free from sufferings. Let noble thoughts come to us from every side.

Namaste 🙏

Rabindranath Mohanty

1368, Brahmeswar Patna

Bhubaneswar-751018

Mob- 9439749074, Email- rnmiob@gmail.com

IGNORANCE IS GREAT SIN
Forgiveness
Renunciation
Love
Restraint
Truth
Practice
Service
SURRENDERING TO TRUTH
Divya Darshan